A Manager's Guide to Newsletters: Communicating for Results

Robert F. Abbott

Word Engines Press

Airdrie, Canada

A Manager's Guide to Newsletters: Communicating for Results
Copyright© 2001 by Word Engines Press
All rights reserved

Canadian Cataloguing in Publication Data

Abbott, Robert F.
 A manager's guide to newsletters
 Includes bibliographical references and index.
 ISBN 0-9683287-2-5 (pbk)
 1. Communication in management. 2. Newsletters. I. Title.
 HF5549.5.C62A22 2001   658.4'55   C98-910997-6

Calgary Quality Council Faxletter © 1995 Quality Council of Alberta

Inside News © 1997 Transcontinental Printing

The Sovereign Report © 1997 The Sovereign General Insurance Company

4 6 8 9 7 5 3

For
Irene and Malcolm Abbott
and, in memory of
Irma and Hector Davies

Contents

Preface i
Introduction 1
Newsletters:
    The Sovereign Report 9
    Inside News 15
    Calgary Quality Council Faxletter 23

Strategy
1. Why newsletters? Why now? 27
2. Your needs and objectives 37
3. Meeting reader needs 47

Tactics
4. Willing and able readers? 59
5. Selecting content 71
6. Presentation tactics 81
7. How often? How many pages? 93

Administration
8. Editorial boards 105
9. Newsletter processes and scheduling 117
10. Newsletter budgets 129
11. Media relations 139
12. Generating article ideas 149

Evaluation
13. Profiling readers 163
14. Costs and returns 175
15. Assessing performance 185

Appendixes
Glossary 193
Further reading 197
Index 201
About the author 210

List of figures

Figure i–1: An integrated newsletter 2

Figure 1–1: Supply and demand elements 30

Figure 2–1: The newsletter loop 38

Figure 3–1: Consumer decision model 49

Figure 3–2: The newsletter loop + decision model 51

Figure 4–1: Newsletter loop (Figure 2–1) 60

Figure 4–2: Willingness to read and the newsletter loop 61

Figure 4–3: Ability to read and the newsletter loop .64

Figure 5–1: The shared environment 72

Figure 7–1: Willingness and ability to respond in the newsletter loop 94

Figure 8–1: Editorial boards in the newsletter loop 106

Figure 8–2: Editorial board representation 113

Figure 9–1: Newsletter processes 118

Figure 9–2: Scheduling 126

Figure 10–1: Budgets 134

Figure 11–1: Media relations in the newsletter loop 141

Figure 11–2: Characteristics of a good news article 144

Figure 12–1: The shared environment (Figure 5–1) 150

Preface

The objective of this book is to help you manage a newsletter. Anyone can produce a newsletter, but an effective newsletter, one that serves your needs and those of the people with whom you communicate, takes more than a set of writing and designing skills. It takes knowledge of management; more specifically, the art and science of newsletter management.

It's art because it taps your creativity to develop effective strategies and tactics. Yes, we normally associate creativity with the writing and designing of newsletters, but a creative mind is equally important in managing for maximized value, particularly when developing strategy and tactics.

It's science in the sense that we want to publish effective newsletters based on a body of methodically arranged knowledge, not guesswork. When I began working on this book, the state of newsletter science was more or less summed up in the phrase "Write for your readers." Good advice, but far too vague when you sit down to work on a newsletter.

A Manager's Guide to Newsletters: Communicating for Results gives you this knowledge, along with the tools and instruction you need to plan and publish without guessing what it means to "Write for your readers." It deals with the practical issues involved in publishing a newsletter that serves your needs and the needs of the people with whom you want to communicate.

Taken together, the art and science of newsletter publishing add up to a system for publishing newsletters, newsletters that influence readers and improve results.

What you'll find, and what you won't

Here, you'll find useful advice that helps you create or refocus a newsletter: advice that leads you step-by-step through the management issues. You'll find out

- Whether a newsletter is the right medium for your purposes
- How to express your objectives as reader responses
- How to understand and meet reader needs
- How to select content that serves your needs and reader needs
- How to present that content
- How to decide on frequency (how often to publish) and number of pages

In addition, a section on administration provides information on managing a newsletter once it's being published regularly. And a section on evaluation will help you assess how well your newsletter is performing.

As you may have surmised by now, this is not a book about writing, editing, desktop publishing, or newsletter design. A number of other books cover those topics, and cover them well. I recommend that you buy at least one of them if you plan to be a hands-on publisher. But before writing or designing, be sure you've covered the management issues – planning, administration, and evaluation.

Using this book

The book assumes you are a busy person: one who wants to pick up the key points quickly, or one who needs a fast refresher before an editorial board meeting. The *Strategy* and *Tactics* sections have been structured with that in mind.

- For a very quick overview of the main points, simply read the summary at the beginning of each chapter in these two sections. **You'll be able to identify the summaries, because they're in a different typeface.**
- For more depth, you can read the summary and the real-life examples at the end of each chapter in the *Strategy* and *Tactics* sections. The examples have been purposely segregated from the main body to make them quickly and easily accessible.
- Of course, you can read it all: summary, main body, and examples. That's the approach I'd recommend. If you do read it all, you'll not only understand the issues more thoroughly, but you'll also be better equipped to think through the challenges posed by your own newsletter.

For whom?

While the book should help anyone responsible for a newsletter, I wrote it with managers, owner-managers, and administrators in mind. But that doesn't limit its usefulness. Anyone responsible for newsletter publishing, including newsletter editors, can apply the principles described here.

In the same vein, the book addresses issues from the perspective of a large organization, rather than a small one. For example, I've assumed that one set of managers determines the mission, another decides on the objectives of departments, a third manages the newsletter, and a separate staff of journalists does the actual editorial and publishing work. You, on the other hand, may own a small business and be responsible for all those roles, and wondering whether this book has any relevance for you. It does. The principles and applications described here should be relevant to any organization, including small ones. The processes will be different, obviously, but the issues will be the same.

Acknowledgements

Much of what you'll read in this book reflects what I've learned from my clients, people who regularly communicate with customers, employees, and members. Some of them must be named here — without their important contributions this book literally would not have been possible. Frank Meyer and Shirley Ingstrup of the Computer Modelling Group; Bob Morgan, Patricia Meadows, and Peter Parkin of The Sovereign General Insurance Company; and Neil LaRocque, Wayne Martyn, and John Dempster of Transcontinental Printing – each has my profound thanks.

Special thanks also go to Bill Kurchak, my partner in The Newsletter Company. He originally suggested a book about newsletters, and he made many contributions, both intellectual and logistical, toward its completion. Thanks also to Jacqueline Turner Kurchak for her contributions, and to the online readers who provided comments after reading sample chapters at the Manager's Guide Web site on the Internet.

In preparing this book for publication, I was fortunate to have the assistance of very capable professionals. My thanks in particular to Dan Wilson of The Editor's DeskTop, who provided a steady and steadying editor's hand.

Thanks to Transcontinental Printing, The Sovereign General Insurance Company, and the Quality Council of Alberta for permission to reprint the newsletters included with this book. Copyright to these publications remains with them.

And most of all, thanks to my family – Ruth, Scott, Lisa, and Brendan – for their longstanding patience and tolerance while this project dragged on over many years.

Introduction

When I opened my mail this morning, I found a newsletter with my electricity bill. Yesterday, one came with my bank statement. And your experience is probably much the same: a regular flow of unsolicited newsletters. They've quietly become fixtures in our lives.

But do these newsletters change the way you think or act? Are you more likely to buy something from a company that sends you one? Will you be a more active member of a non-profit organization that sends you a membership newsletter? Questions like these concern people who are responsible for non-subscription newsletters, because newsletters have little value unless they influence the way you respond to some issue, product, or service.

Perhaps you publish a newsletter yourself. If you do, you'll understand how hard it is to know whether you're doing the right thing. Of course, lots of books and articles tell you how to write and lay out a newsletter, but until now there's been nothing that answers the strategic and tactical questions managers ask: "Should we publish a newsletter?" "What kind of content should we put into it?" "How many pages should it have?" "How do we know whether what we're doing is working?"

As the owner and manager of a company that develops and publishes custom, non-subscription newsletters, I frequently hear questions like these. Some come from clients, others from acquaintances thinking about starting newsletters, and yet others from managers who already publish newsletters, but wonder whether they're having the desired effect on readers.

A Manager's Guide to Newsletters: Communicating for Results answers those managerial questions, and it does so in management language, using concepts and words with which managers routinely work and think.

The bigger picture

Let's start by identifying newsletters as tools that help managers, owners, administrators, and others communicate with stakeholders. We use the word stakeholders to describe groups of persons on whom the organization depends in some way (such as employees, customers, and members).

In this book, newsletters have no independent function – they're the tools of other purposes. In large organizations, they help individual departments accomplish objectives. In smaller organizations they serve the goals of the entire firm or association. And those objectives or goals, once accomplished, help the organization move toward the fulfillment of its mission.

All of this means that a newsletter's purposes and operations should align and connect with the broader mandate of the whole organization. An overview of this relationship between the newsletter and the rest of the organization is shown in the figure below. In it, you'll find the following elements:

- *Mission* refers to the purpose or ultimate goal of the entire organization.
- *Objective* means a departmental or functional goal that, if achieved, helps the organization fulfill its mission.
- *Strategy* sets out how the newsletter will help the department achieve its objective. Note that there can be more than one strategy for a given objective.
- *Tactics* flesh out the strategy, explaining how the relatively abstract strategy will be converted into concrete plans and operations.
- *Administration* refers to the management and supervision of work done in the course of ongoing publishing.
- *Evaluation* is assessing how effectively the newsletter has moved the department toward its objective. This knowledge feeds back into the setting of updated strategies, tactics, and tasks.

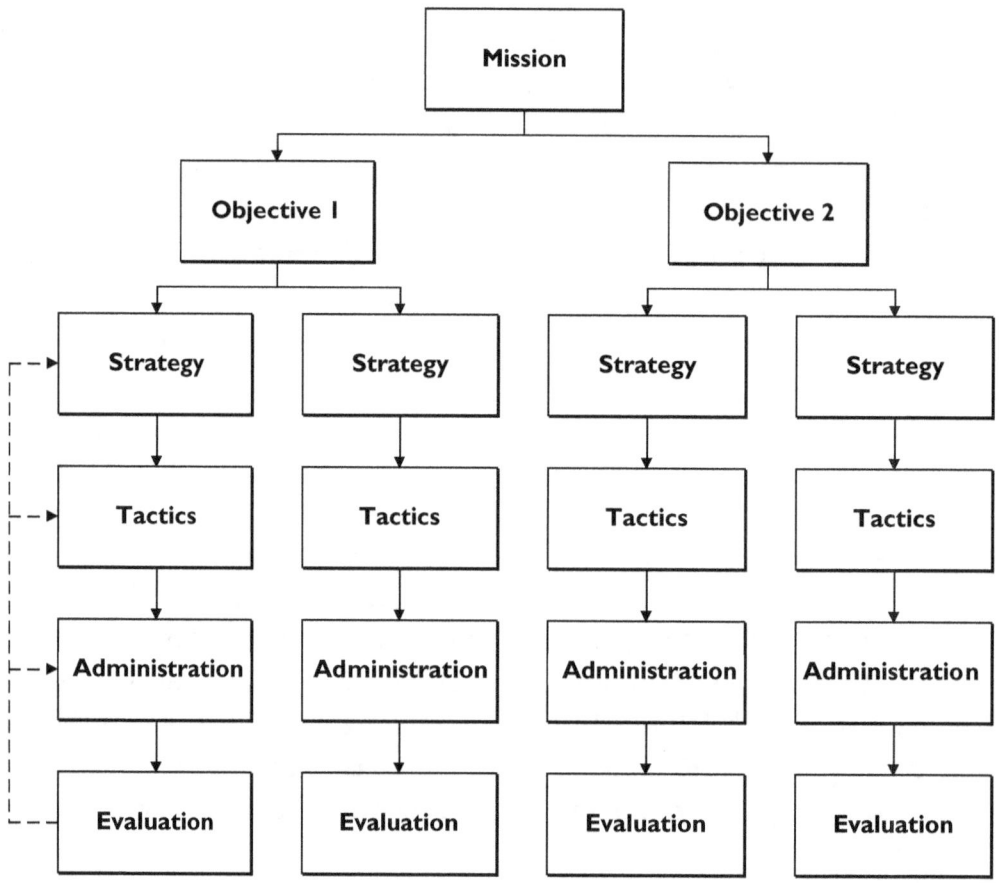

Figure i–1

As the figure suggests, all of these elements taken together comprise a system.

The structure of this book follows the structure of Figure i–1. It takes, as givens, the *Mission* and the *Organizational Objectives*. It starts with *Strategy*, then goes through *Tactics, Administration,* and *Evaluation*. One section is allocated to each of these issues, and within each section, individual chapters deal with specific subjects.

Strategy

In this section, we ask the *what* questions: What will we do to achieve our objectives for the newsletter?

> *Chapter 1* looks at the mass media, including newsletters, as vehicles for persuasion. Within that context, it further develops criteria that will help you decide whether a newsletter is the appropriate medium for you.
>
> *Chapter 2* deals with objectives for the newsletter, expressed in terms of reader responses.
>
> *Chapter 3* addresses the issue of reader needs, and explains how newsletters can help readers achieve their goals.

Tactics

Strategy dealt with *what* we want to do. The Tactics section deals with *how*. We work with four tactical issues:

1. The types of subject matter
2. How we present these subjects
3. How often we publish
4. The number of pages or words

> *Chapter 4* does not deal directly with tactics, but develops two concepts that underpin them. Those concepts are the *willingness* and *ability* of readers – their willingness and ability to read our newsletter.
>
> *Chapter 5* uses the concept of reader willingness to determine what subject matter, or content, should go into a newsletter. This is the first tactical issue.
>
> *Chapter 6* explains how to use three types of reader characteristics – involvement, emotion, and consistency – to make choices about presentation styles.

Chapter 7 shows how to base frequency and page count decisions on readers' willingness and ability to *respond* to the message we send out in the newsletter.

Administration

In this section, we look at some processes that managers will supervise, and at the supervisory process itself.

Chapter 8 introduces editorial boards, which are teams or committees that make policy, as well as supervise and support the newsletter staff.

Chapter 9 outlines the processes involved in publishing a newsletter. We also look at the publishing process in reverse, to create publishing schedules.

Chapter 10 takes us to newsletter budgets, providing spending parameters and describing the many different types of costs.

Chapter 11 looks at extending your influence by using a newsletter for media relations.

Chapter 12 picks up where Chapter 5 left off. Here, we offer some processes and ideas to help you develop content from within the framework set out in Chapter 5.

Evaluation

No managerial process is complete without a systematic evaluation of the work done, and supervising a newsletter is no exception.

Chapter 13 provides techniques for classifying readers according to demographic, pyschographic, or other key characteristics.

Chapter 14 uses simple arithmetic and formulas, to develop ways of assessing the financial contribution a newsletter can make to an organization.

Chapter 15 outlines a strategy and procedure for assessing the performance of a newsletter. It also concludes the book, summing up the major strategic and tactical issues we've addressed.

For example...

This book includes three newsletters that I've helped start and publish. At the end of each chapter in the *Strategy* and *Tactics* sections, you'll find a brief discussion based on these newsletters, to illustrate the points made in that chapter. As noted, the examples have been kept separate from the discussion in each chapter for your convenience.

There are three examples, one each for marketing, employee, and membership newsletters. The organizations and their newsletters are

>   **Marketing newsletter:** *The Sovereign Report*, published by The Sovereign General Insurance Company.
>   **Employee newsletter:** *Inside News*, published by Transcontinental Printing Inc.
>   **Membership newsletter:** *Calgary Quality Council Faxletter*, published by the Calgary Quality Council.

Here's some background information that will help explain the purpose and history of each of these newsletters.

Marketing newsletter: *The Sovereign Report*

The Sovereign General Insurance Company (The Sovereign) is a leading Canadian property and casualty insurance company. It underwrites business, home, auto, and specialty lines of insurance. It does this through a select group of insurance brokers located throughout Canada.

Insurance companies (also called insurers) have three main channels through which they distribute their products (policies) to consumers:

1. By direct marketing, whether through phone, mail, or mass media advertising
2. Through exclusive agencies that carry only their own policies
3. Through the traditional channel of independent agents and brokers, which is what The Sovereign uses.

Independent agents and brokers buy for, or represent, consumers and select from among the policies offered by perhaps a dozen insurers to find the best match between consumer and insurer. As the word broker suggests, the independents add value by acting as intermediaries between insurers and consumers. In some ways, insurers and brokers have a relationship like that between a manufacturer (insurer) and a retailer (broker).

These relationships are dynamic. Brokers change their stable of insurers from time to time, because they're looking for a mix that better reflects their clients' needs, because they're dissatisfied with the service or products they get from an insurer, because one insurer offers better commissions than another, or for other reasons. Insurers also make changes from time to time, as they look for better representation in a given community, seek better sales organizations or better risks, experience disagreements with individual brokers over professional issues, or discover other reasons for changing.

While some tension is therefore unavoidable, insurers and brokers still must work together to compete with the other distribution channels: direct marketers and exclusive agencies. And, in recent years, there has been concern in the industry about the entry of other players, particularly banks, into this already competitive industry.

One way The Sovereign maintains its good relationship with brokers and addresses competition from other channels is by publishing *The Sovereign Report*. This four-page newsletter has been mailed to about 500 brokers and agents every two months (bi-monthly), since the first issue in February, 1990. In addition to the four regular pages of text, there is often a one-page (one- or two-sided) *Sovereign Report Supplement*. While the newsletter proper focuses on non-promotional editorial content, the *Supplement* provides a forum for discussion of products and services offered by The Sovereign. It also provides information that could help reduce claims, and consequently reduce The Sovereign's costs.

The newsletter was launched by now-retired Vice President, Marketing Bob Morgan and the author. Shortly afterward, Patricia Meadows joined the informal editorial board. Peter Parkin, Vice President, Branch Operations, now supervises it. He also writes Page 4 and selects material for the *Supplement*. The other three pages are researched and written by the author. Layout and design are handled by a third party.

The Sovereign Report also is published in French, a translation of the English language version. The French edition goes mainly to brokers representing The Sovereign in the province of Quebec.

Employee newsletter: *Inside News*

Transcontinental Printing Inc. (TCP) is a division of G.T.C. Transcontinental Group Ltd., one of North America's largest and fastest-growing printing companies. In addition to its printing businesses, G.T.C. has used its technological sophistication to move aggressively into related information technologies and businesses such as CD–ROMs.

The Western Regional Division of TCP operates three web press printing plants in Western Canada and one at Miami Valley, Ohio. It sells and distributes print products throughout Western Canada, Washington state, and the Midwestern U.S. The four plants produce newspaper advertising inserts and advertising flyers.

The main customers for these products are major retailing chains, which face significant challenges of their own. Among the most important are new technologies such as electronic catalogs, new competitors such as Internet marketers, changing channel strategies among manufacturers, and ferocious price competition. In response, Transcontinental Printing has become an industry leader in the application of advanced technologies. It also has adopted new sales and management strategies that enhance its own competitiveness and that of its customers.

To keep employees informed about changes in their plants and in the industry, TCP's Western Division publishes *Inside News*. Published bi-monthly, it provides technical and managerial information, as well as news about people and events.

The newsletter began in October 1991, under the direction of John Dempster and Neil LaRocque, and supported a Total Quality Management initiative. After the first issue, the editorial team grew to include Wayne Martyn and the author. Over the following two years, the newsletter evolved and grew to provide other information, including news about corporate direction and accomplishments, health and safety issues, industry and technology, the challenges facing customers, and news about people in each of the plants.

In January, 1994 it became *Inside News*, an eight-page newsletter published bi-monthly. Under the direction of Neil LaRocque and Wayne Martyn, the editorial board began surveying readers (the 800+ employees and managers in the four plants) annually, and the results of those surveys have dictated the content and treatment of subjects in the newsletter since then.

Membership newsletter: *Calgary Quality Council Faxletter*

The Calgary Quality Council (CQC) was a non-profit organization founded in 1992 to promote Total Quality Management and Quality Assurance. In 1995, it merged with the Quality Council of Alberta (QCA), to become the Calgary chapter of the QCA.

To promote Total Quality Management (TQM) and Quality Assurance (QA), the Council undertook a number of initiatives. These included public presentations and forums, joint events with other organizations that held similar mandates, and a monthly newsletter, the *Calgary Quality Council Faxletter*.

The *Faxletter* was used to maintain contact with existing members, to promote membership to non-members, and for liaison with other organizations. This two-page newsletter was under the supervision of Directors Lorne Tetarenko and Ed Tickles, as well as the author (the President of the Council).

As the name suggests, the *Faxletter* was distributed by facsimile; no printed version was published, except for a few laser-printed copies mailed to people without fax machines. For the Council, this method of distribution was a necessity, since it was unable to afford conventional printing and distribution.

Once tried, though, the fax method was found to have a number of advantages, and it probably would have continued, even if funding for printing and mailing had become available.

At the time of its final issue, the *Faxletter* was being faxed to about 250 persons, including members, prospective members, and representatives of other organizations.

Note:

For technical reasons, *The Sovereign Report* and *Inside News* have been reconstructed; they have not been printed on the original paper stocks, nor do you see the colors of the originals. For those reasons, they look slightly different than the original versions, and in the case of *Inside News* two birth announcements are not included here. Otherwise, you're seeing what the original recipient saw. The *Calgary Quality Council Faxletter,* though, was distributed by fax, and so you see a close representation of the original in that case.

Volume 8, No. 6   November/December 1997

No Millennium Parties for Computers

While some people may have started talking about millennium parties, people who manage computers foresee anything but a party when the calendar changes from 1999 to 2000. We're referring, of course, to the so-called 'millennium bug,' which leaves some software unable to make the transition in dating from the 1900s to the 2000s.

For those who thought insurance would pick up the cost of damages, there may be another surprise that won't have them blowing their noisemakers. *Computerworld* magazine reports that many insurers are making changes to general property and liability policies to exclude year 2000 damages.

On this subject, there's good news for procrastinators—while many companies and organizations are addressing the need to recode millions of lines of software programming, others are content to defer the problem for a few years.

At the Montgomery Mutual Insurance Co., the Information Systems department tricked its mainframe, and by doing so, bought itself some time—up to 31 years worth. The calendar for 1997 is the same as the calendar for 1969, so the company shifted all dates in the system back 28 years.

Software then automatically converts any dates from the mainframe back to their current values, and users don't notice the change. And, as the mainframe is phased out, the problem is phased out. Best of all, this 'solution' cost Montgomery about half a million dollars, compared with $4 million for a more conventional solution.

As an official at the company notes, they were already accustomed to 'lying' to their mainframe. For example, the mainframe provides access to what it believes are terminals, but they're really client and server applications, including World Wide Web browsers. (Insurers plan limitations on Y2K coverage, *Computerworld*, September 1, 1997; and Insurer 'lies' to avoid year 2000 costs, *Computerworld*, July 28, 1997)

Season's Greetings

All of us at The Sovereign would like to wish you the best for the coming holiday season. Again this year we will make contributions to charities in cities across the country, rather than send out cards. While we regret not being able to send you a personalized greeting, we know you support our efforts to help the less fortunate, for whom this time of year is especially difficult.

A member of the Co-operators Group of Companies

Proposals that sell

We'd all like to sell without them, but proposals are a fact of life. And, if we can make them more effective, we've got a competitive advantage that makes the time spent on them worthwhile. Sales consultant Art Siegel says a winning proposal contains six parts.

1. Introduction. This sets the tone of the whole proposal, and does so by articulating the prospect's goal or goals, by showing you've created a custom document based on those goals, and by listing the issues you will cover.

2. Condition. Here, you deal with the prospect's situation in detail, repeating the key information you've received, or referring to other information that the prospect has given you.

3. Problem. Builds on the Condition section, by describing in detail the barriers that prevent the prospect from achieving the goal or goals listed above. It also tells the prospect that you understand the nature and scope of the problem/opportunity.

4. Solution. This section, the most extensive, is made up of three parts:
   - An introduction to your capabilities—those specifically related to the prospects's goal or problems. This should be no longer than one page.
   - Your solution—which should include a description of the products or services you will apply; schedules; and prices.
   - The next steps to be taken—a list which should focus on getting the prospect to say 'yes' to the first step. That, in turn, should be de facto agreement to the entire proposal.

5. Validation. Provide testimonials, references for the prospect to call, and brief descriptions of solutions provided for other organizations.

6. Backgrounders. Supporting information about your company, such as its history, profiles of key officers and employees, and customer lists.

Don't underestimate the importance of sections 1, 2, and 3. These sections create and build prospect interest, as well as involvement and agreement, before posing the solution. Having read those first three sections, the prospect should sense clearly that you understand the need, and you're prepared to address it. Similarly, the Validation and Backgrounders sections address the potential problem of buyer's remorse.

Notice how this format creates a flow—it starts by describing a goal, and its context, moves to a solution and supports it with specific plans and commitments, and winds up with reassurances. (Double Your Sales, *$alesDoctors Magazine*, September 1, 1997)

A tool for focusing

If you find your organization getting sidetracked, give some thought to developing a mission statement. A good one will articulate your purpose, goals, and values—all of which will help you stay focused. Develop principles you can use every day to guide yourself and your employees. Write it in simple words and concepts, so everyone can understand it. Involve as many employees as possible, especially by setting up a consultation process, then test-drive a temporary draft. And take a look at the mission statements of your competitors when possible, to see what works and doesn't work. With a good mission statement in place, you'll also find it easier to make quick decisions, increase teamwork, and empower employees to take reasonable risks. (Management: You can Keep Your Staff on the Competitive Track, *Your Company* magazine, August 1997)

It's not just the Post Office

While we're all concerned about mail disruptions at the Post Office, modern technology also makes us vulnerable to disruptions of electronic communications. A recent story from Fredericton, New Brunswick describes how 30,000 customers of NBTel temporarily lost their e-mail and Internet access because of one mail bomb. With software that can send tens of thousands of rogue e-mail messages at one click of a mouse, Internet service providers (and their customers) can be hit with severe disruptions. In this case, the havoc was caused by one 14 year old boy. And while providers respond with new safeguards to incidents like this one, the system can never be entirely bomb-proofed, since the 'bad guys' look on improved defences as new challenges for their hacking skills. All of which means you and your clients should not take the electronic mail system for granted, even after you've figured out how to use it. ('Our system just went bleccch,' *Cybersun,* August 19, 1997)

Takeover insurance

Mergers and acquisitions, once again, are big business for lawyers, investment bankers and stockbrokers. And, defensive advice, too. With that in mind, a British firm has been selling coverage for the cost of anti-takeover advice. TOI has insured more than 70 mostly small, publicly-owned British firms since 1990, and now is moving into the U.S. It assumes that a company with a market capitalization of 30 million pounds would pay out 500,000 pounds to investment bankers, lawyers, accountants, and public relations people for a successful defence to a hostile bid. It offers coverage of that expense for an annual premium of 3.5% to 6% of the amount covered. Criteria for premiums include market share, industry sector, percentage of shares held by management, and the names of investors on the share register. (Gekko insurance, *The Economist,* July 19, 1997)

Dear Friends:

Three fleeting years of relative rate stability have led to this—what is being described in some sectors of the country as the most insane insurance market ever witnessed. And this, in a low interest rate economy that offers investment returns that are at times volatile and unpredictable.

Sure—let's chop rates to the bone; that makes real good sense. The industry's historical return on equity really makes a "strong" statement that the product is over-priced.

It's a "heart-warming" experience for an underwriter to watch an account she's serviced loyally for several years being re-marketed by the broker due to some very basic loss control recommendations. An underwriter gets another real boost when a broker never bothers to call back on that new account because she just asked too many questions. It doesn't take long for underwriters to question what value their skills really bring to the table—deaf, blind and dumb gets the business over analytical, inquisitive and probing. Knowledge is a drawback.

What's sad is that what drives certain players in our industry to ignore all the essential fundamentals of this intriguing business, also drives others to follow suit out of the quest for survival. In the end, primary companies and reinsurers pay through massive underwriting losses and insolvencies; well-trained professional underwriters pay because they forget and no longer believe what they learned; brokers pay through loss of market and of credibility with their clients—and of course the client who we're ultimately all supposed to be concerned about, always pays.

But, there is hope—hope that brokers like the one several of us had dinner with the other night continue to thrive and survive. This broker believes in and practises all of the fundamentals that we believe in—a true professional. Lowering the price without justification is the last thing on his mind; providing stable professional service and advice is the driving motivation in his operation. It's funny—he and quite a few others like him across the country seem to be the only ones who have clients who don't expect an unsolicited 60% price reduction on renewal. Even stranger, with these brokers our underwriters actually get their questions answered and have no problems getting recommendations complied with.

Go figure.

Peter A. Parkin
Vice President, Branch Operations

HEAD OFFICE	**Vancouver**	**Winnipeg**	**Halifax**
2200, 855 - 2nd St. SW	1400, 1095 West Pender Street	1009, 201 Portage Avenue	7th Floor – 5121 Sackville Street
Calgary, Alberta T2P 4J8	Vancouver, B. C. V6E 2M6	Winnipeg, Manitoba R3B 3K6	Halifax. Nova Scotia B3J 1K1
(403) 298-4200	(604) 602-8300	(204) 982-1260	(902) 492-0234
Marine Subsidiary	**Calgary**	**Toronto**	**St. John's**
Harlock Williams Lemon Ltd.	2200, 855 - 2nd St. SW	840, 121 King Street West	202, 35 Blackmarsh Road
701, 890 West Pender	Calgary, Alberta T2P 4J8	Toronto, Ontario M5H 3T9	St. John's. Newfoundland A1E 1S4
Vancouver. B.C. V6C 1K5	(403) 298-4290	(416) 365-1818	(709) 739-9601
(604) 669-7745	**Edmonton**	**Montreal**	
	2350, 10060 Jasper Avenue	800 René-Lévesque blvd. West, Suite 1410	
	Edmonton, Alberta T5J 3R8	Montréal. Quebec H3B 1X9	
	(403) 423-2300	(514) 395-8100	

THE SOVEREIGN REPORT SUPPLEMENT

A Word to the Wise

Winter's coming and once again we'll all be slip-sliding through our daily activities.

This is a great time for brokers to review with their clients the duties imposed upon them by law to keep premises as safe as possible. This is true whether the condition exists outside or inside; but this time of year, "outside" grabs the headlines.

There are two cases that illustrate both the dangers and the expectations of society through the eyes of the law; one case deals with outside hazards and one inside—and the results were as opposite as the locales.

In *Arial v. 882657 Ontario Inc.*, the plaintiff had slipped on a small patch of black ice and fell down an outside flight of stairs while coming out of the defendant's restaurant. The restaurant had a system in place to deal with customer safety, but the Court found it to be vague and unreliable. Apparently the restaurant cook had cleared and salted the stairs about two hours before the restaurant had opened that day. After that, it was the server's responsibility to check the stairs and clear them as needed. The defendant could not produce any evidence that demonstrated that the server had made any effort to do so that morning. The court found the defendant restaurant 60% liable.

In *Fauser v. Westfair Foods Ltd.*, the plaintiff was a 39 year old woman who slipped and fell inside the defendant's grocery store. The defendant store had a formal contract in place with a janitorial service for the night-time hours right up until opening time each day. On the day in question it could easily be shown that the janitorial team had been there during the night with a final inspection of the floor 15 minutes after the store had opened. The store also had a policy that throughout the day, commencing 1/2 hour after the night cleaners had finished, the entire floor area had to be swept every 20 minutes.

In this case the plaintiff action was dismissed. The Court found that the defendants exercised the required degree of care by being able to clearly show a policy of inspecting and cleaning, and a system of carrying out the policy. Even though it was determined that the plaintiff had slipped on sugar that was on the floor, the existence of that substance did not detract from the reasonable care of the defendant store.

These two cases highlight the importance of occupiers to not only have a documented system of frequent maintenance and inspection, but also to make certain it is consistently adhered to.

November/December 1997

A member of the Co-operators Group of Companies

A Publication of the Western Regional Employees

Volume 4, Issue 3　　　Transcontinental Printing　　　July 1997

Brand Names or Generics?

The only difference is the cost

Generic drugs are really brand-name products that the generic firms are allowed to copy, once the period of market exclusivity for original medicines expires. Because these pharmaceutical companies have no research and development costs, they can sell their products at much lower prices, sometimes as much as 50% less.

Asking for generic drugs is the responsible thing to do, especially considering that you have nothing to lose with regard to quality or effectiveness, because generic drugs have to meet the same standards as brand-name medicines. So when you need medication, ask your doctor to prescribe generic drugs if they are available.

We have to do what we can to cut costs. Buying generic drugs is a step in the right direction.

Why pay more for the same thing?

One and half years accident-free

Goss C-150 at Miami Valley Publishing

On May 31, 1997 the 210 people at Miami Valley reached a major milestone—one and a half years without a lost-time accident. That's a total of 548 consecutive days.

It's a remarkable achievement, one that Environment and Safety Manager Darryll Heck attributes to the efforts of employees, supervisors, and management, as well as a good program.

That program is Dupont's STOP, which is focused at the supervisory level in Miami Valley. It's a non-disciplinary program, designed to eliminate unsafe conditions and unsafe acts by employees To eliminate these unsafe situations, supervisors audit

Continued on Page 4

Inside

Winnipeg: The Great Blizzard 3
Vancouver: Training days 4
Calgary: New Prepress space 5
Miami Valley 4
Pension fund administration 7
Inserting finishes the job 8

What's New?

Impact of mill mergers

Merger and acquisition activities by pulp and paper companies in Canada have been on the rise. That means fewer companies in the paper business. And, what does that mean to paper supply and prices?

Generally, everyone agrees that prices will be more stable, especially more than they've been over the past few years. However, some think that there will be some cyclical pricing, even though the big producers will have more influence on the market.

Still, fewer companies shouldn't mean a monopoly market for the producers. That's because paper is becoming part of the global market, with competition coming from other countries. And, if there's no monopoly, it means printers won't be at the mercy of paper producers.

There's already been a consolidation in the paper distribution business. There are now just four major players in Canada: Unisource, Buntin Reid, Coast Papers, and Graphic Papers. (Canadian Printer) •

Interactive safety

The Internet, and especially the World Wide Web part of it, may become an important part of your health and safety committee. We learned about one interesting application from the Environmental Advisor, a newsletter published by the National Association of Printers and Lithographers (NAPL).

The newsletter cites a survey of safety professionals, and the top 10 issues which get most of their time and attention:
1. Personal protective equipment
2. Ergonomics
3. OSHA's Hard Communication Standard
4. Bloodborne pathogens
5. Confined spaces
6. Defensive driving
7. Lockout/tagout
8. Environmental protection
9. Chemical handling
10. Respiratory protection.

But, are those the right issues on which to focus? OSHA, the Occupational Safety and Health Administration in the United States, now offers an interactive way to find out. Companies can dial into the OSHA Web site, click on 'Statistics & Data,' and enter data about the number of employees, the state where the company is located, and the industry's SIC code.

What comes back is a report on what inspectors found in visits to companies in the same size range, in the same state, and in the same industry. That, in turn, helps safety committees find out what violations inspectors are finding in visits to similar companies.

You can find the NAPL web site at www.napl.org (Environmental Advisor) •

New retail tech

Add the term 'data mining' to your vocabulary. It refers to a new class of software that will be very important to the retail industry in the near future.

This software rapidly sorts through enormous databases (now called 'data warehouses'). While it's going through those databases, it uses statistical and artificial intelligence techniques to look for patterns that might never be found otherwise. Conventional databases searches don't use those techniques, and normally don't find patterns unless human beings describe them first.

The phone company MCI uses data mining to keep its best customers. To do that, it's computers go through marketing data on 140 million households, and evaluate them on as many as 10,000 individual attributes. So far, it's found 22 key statistical profiles.

For major retailers, this technology means many new marketing opportunities. Wal-Mart, for example, uses data mining to predict demand for the thousands of items in each store, and for combinations of items that consumers tend to buy in one visit. (Business Week) •

Your Local Editors...

Vancouver	Calgary	Winnipeg	Miami Valley
Marilyn Young	Neil LaRocque	Dave Craig	John Meadows
(604) 540-2333	(403) 258-3788	(204) 633-8890	(513) 879-5678

n Winnipeg

centimetres (almost 2 feet) of wind driven snow fell on Winnipeg during the Great Blizzard of April 5, 1997.

After it ended, the few stragglers that made it in began the cleanup. Here, we see Heather Cornwell of Prepress doing her share. The front entrance was completely blown in and it looked like an all day job. Good thing Heather was on a 12 hour shift (and had a front-end loader to help).

Fortunately, the Great Flood of '97, which followed soon after the Great Blizzard, did not affect us.

Dan (The Legend) Sawicz Retires

On April 16, Dan Sawicz ended his 15 year career here. He joined us from the recently closed Winnipeg Tribune, and worked as a platemaker here for many years. He was trained as a stripper and worked the 12 hour shift until his retirement.

A small party was held, honouring him with gifts for his service to the company. Good luck, Dan. Come and visit soon.

Congratulations!

to Ed Hodgert (Prepress) and Jocelyne Dufault who were married on June 21. Best wishes from all of us!

The Great Blizzard of '97

In Vancouver

Training update

In preparation for the arrival of summer, and summer holidays, a significant amount of training has had to take place over the last 2 months. We have brought in a wraith of summer relief help which has created a vast amount of training.

By adding staff to our crews, we are then able to upgrade employees to help cover for those employees taking vacation. These employees who are being upgraded also have been receiving training that will assist them in their new roles.

Covering for summer holidays in this fashion presents many challenges, especially for the crews involved. It also creates many opportunities for training and promotion of our employees in the future.

Canadian Occupational Health and Safety Week

We participated in the Canadian Occupational Health and Safety Week, held from June 2nd – 6th.

COHS week is intended to increase awareness of the importance of Occupational Health and Safety, and ultimately to reduce injuries and illness in the workplace.

The theme for this year's safety week was "Managing Safely."

Congratulations

Congratulations to Chad Lynch and Coralie, on the birth of their daughter Riley, on April 14.

In Miami Valley

Accident-free

Continued from Page 1

the plant regularly. Darryll says, "People have a tendency to relax, so you have to keep checking, even if it's at a lesser level."

He adds, "Before we began using STOP we had less than 50% compliance with rules, but now we have 97% or 98% compliance. That's due to continuing close attention to rules and procedures."

STOP was introduced to Miami Valley in April 1995, and began with training of supervisors and managers, which lasted until the end of September 1995. Training of employees followed, beginning in January 1996, and lasted through March. They were introduced to the principles of STOP, through supervisors. Now, there are monthly meetings to cover Occupational Safety and Health Administration rules and regulations. There's also a strong commitment to safety by management and members of the safety committee, which is made up of employees.

Darryll adds, "I'd like to thank everyone for their cooperation in achieving this outstanding safety record. To the employees for their cooperation, and to the supervisors and management for their commitment, and for making the safety issue manageable."

To acknowledge the safety achievement, 92 gifts were distributed by a drawing to plant employees.

Training at paper mill

Miami Valley's Training Department has conducted two sessions of Heatset Press Training at the Bowater Paper Mill in Calhoun, Tennessee.

The sessions were conducted for paper machine crews, the people who make paper for our presses.

In conjunction with the sessions, the training crews received tours of the paper plant. A video of the Calhoun Mill is available for viewing in training room #3. Take a look at the video—it will help you understand a great deal about one of the most important raw materials we use.

New film inspection process

Pre-press has introduced a new six-step process at the newly remodelled film check-in station. It's a new quality control concept, instituted to double check the accuracy of each piece of film that is output. The steps are:

1. Trimming excess film in preparation for stripping to vinyl.
2. Reading the density of the film to make sure it is within specifications.
3. Measuring the line screen to verify it is at the proper setting.
4. Checking to ensure the markings used to identify each individual negative is correct, and matches the information to be given to Stripping.
5. The film is checked for content, including wording, picture placement, and changes requested by the customer.
6. The film is taped together by pages and placed in an appropriately labeled rack.

At this point, the film is released to Stripping, where the film will be placed on vinyl to prepare it for exposure on a Misomex plate burning machine.

n Calgary

enovations that added new space
) TCP Calgary are nearing
ompletion.

)n the main floor, the new space
rovides room for Prepress to
xpand, and on the floor above, new
ffices for Administration.

hown at the right are photos of the
ew Prepress space.

Congratulations

[Two birth announcements here in
the original version.]

Stress Busters

- Get up 15 minutes earlier in the morning.
- Prepare for the morning— the evening before.
- Simplify, simplify, simplify.
- Every day, do something you really enjoy.
- Schedule a realistic day.
- Allow yourself time for the unexpected.

Thanks to Les Consultants
Sheppell Ltée for these tips, taken
from its information sheet titled
35 proven stress reducers.

Les Consultants Sheppell Ltée is one
of TCP's Employee Assistance
Program consultants, providing
employee counselling services in
Calgary and **Winnipeg.**

1-800-387-4765 (English)

1-800-361-5676 (French)

In **Vancouver,** counselling is available from *interlock Employee and Family Assistance Society* at:

431-8200

In **Miami Valley,** counselling can be received from *Employee Care of Miami Valley and Good Samaritan Hospitals.*

1-800-628-9343

Prepress expands

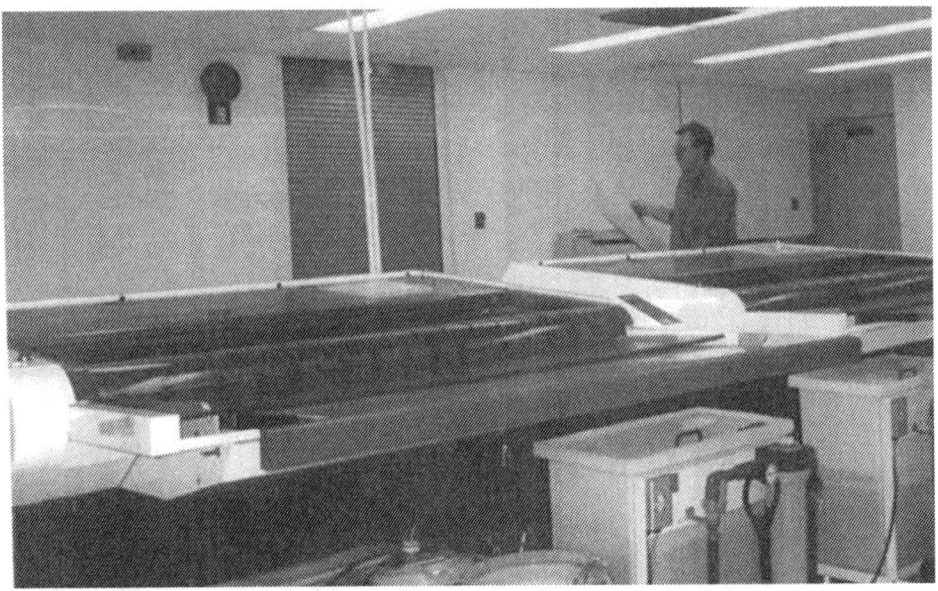

The Future of Print in the Era of the Internet, and Vice Versa

This is an excerpt from a speech by Rémi Marcoux to the Laval [Quebec] Chamber of Commerce and Industry on April 23, 1997.

The speech is one of a number of corporate documents you can access through the Internet, by going to our home page (available in both French and English)

http://transcontinental-gtc.com/

A historic crossroads

Transcontinental stands at the intersection of the oldest technologies still being used today, the printing press, invented by Gutenberg around the year 1440, and one of the most recent, the Internet, which has exploded on the scene in a mere five years.

Over 85% of Transcontinental's current revenues come from printed products: the ones we produce and distribute for clients, and the ones we use for our own publications.

The rest, 15%, comes from our subsidiary Americ Disc, one of the main compact-disc producers in North America, and various other services, including ones related to electronic information and commerce.

I can tell you right now that these percentages are not going to change much in the next few years.

In my opinion, the Internet is not a threat to print, whether one is talking about newspapers, books, flyers, catalogues or magazines. So, to answer the question posed by the title of this presentation, I would say that "in the era of the Internet, we can expect a promising and prosperous future for print."

Why am I convinced that printed products will long continue to be central to Transcontinental's activities? Simply because they will continue to be indispensable to our clients' marketing programs and to consumers.

We can learn from the past

On this point, the past has something to teach us. Television didn't make radio disappear, and radio didn't eliminate newspapers. Each media adjusted to the new reality. For instance, daily newspapers

G.T.C.'s home page on the Internet

started appearing as morning editions, of which there had been only a few in the early sixties.

Inevitably, the world has changed with each new technology, but never in as dramatic a fashion as was predicted.

I would even go so far as to say that the new technologies are creating interesting spinoffs for printers. As you can see for yourselves every day, there are many TV-related publications available on the newsstands. And I'm sure you all remember the prediction that the computer would bring us the paperless office; yet when I look at the invoices from our paper suppliers, the opposite is true: computers have increased the use of paper.

Also, every CD-ROM sold comes with printed material. One of our printers, Ross-Ellis, now does 85% of its sales in compact-disc booklets, a field that it did not even operate in five years ago.

And the American outdoor-clothing manufacturer, Patagonia, which distributes over 500,000 catalogues every year, has seen demand for their catalogues increase, which they attribute to new interest attracted through their Internet site.

What revolution?

Another point: at Transcontinental, we never say the words "Internet" and "revolution" in the same breath.

For us, the Internet is integrated into our basic business philosophy, which is understood and shared by our 7,200 employees: evolve with our customers and anticipate their needs.

So our business model is simple: For Transcontinental, the driving force is the customer. Our role is to help businesses communicate effectively with their consumers.

To achieve this, we have added a whole series of new and innovative products and services over the years....

To read the full text of M. Marcoux's speech, please go to the What's New? page of the G.T.C. Web site, at:

http://transcontinental-gtc.com/

At the site, you can also view a number of other corporate information resources, including recent press releases.

Putting the pieces together

Continued from Page 8

accumulating a pile of pre-determined size, the inserter puts it on the conveyor belt. At the end of the belt, the bundles are jogged, tied, or placed bulk on a skid. Once a skid is completed, Material Handlers pick it up for shipping.

Terryl says inserters use either the pinch method or the lift method. A person using the pinch method pinches a corner of the product to put it in place, while the lift method involves raising the side of the product. "The type that a person uses depends on what's comfortable," says Terryl, "And, that's fine with us as long as the method is ergonomically correct, and meets the customer's request for proper placement of the insert."

Ergonomics first

In the last three years, ergonomic issues have been front and center. That has involved construction of a new inserting belt and table, so inserters stand comfortably while working. Standing properly means working with your forearms parallel to the floor. It also involves training in proper bending and lifting methods. And, inserters now have regular exercise routines throughout their shifts. At the beginning of the shift, it's a seven minute warm-up, and that's followed by a three to five minute exercise routine at the top of every hour.

The results of the ergonomics focus have been very positive. "Many inserters didn't know the repetitive motions were hurting them until they moved the right way, and their aches and pains lessened," says Terryl.

At the beginning of April this year, a cap was imposed on the number of copies per hour, again to decrease repetitive strain injuries. The new limit restricts inserters to 2,500 copies an hour.

Output

The final products of the department include not only inserted materials, but also folded and boxed materials. Folding involves eighth-folding for premium mail, a business that's increased dramatically since Canada Post changed from admail to premium at the beginning of this year. Boxing is handled by the inserters when it can't be done by the presses.

But, inserting remains the big business, with volume ranging from 2.5 million to 4 million copies a week. All done by 78 inserters on 4 shifts, each with two very fast hands. *

Takin' care of business

In this, the final article of our series about pensions for Canadian employees, we look at administration of the plan.

Again, don't hesitate to contact your benefits coordinator about any questions or concerns—they'd be pleased to help. If you're in Miami Valley, please consult with the Human Resources Department.

Who runs the pension plan?

The Transcontinental pension plan is administered by a five-member committee. Of the five members, two (elected for a three year term) represent the participants, two represent the employer (V.P. Finance Human Resources and Controller), and one attends as an independent member (V.P Finance of Laurentian Bank). The pension committee meets at least three times a year to review the administration, meet with Pension Fund Investment Counsel, approve financial statements, and discuss investment policy.

Day-to-day administration of the fund is handled by Transcontinental, which complies with set regulations and accounts for its actions to the pension committee. In order to fulfill its obligations, Transcontinental is assisted by:

- Administrators of the pension plan, who perform terminal calculations, calculate annuities, and maintain the data bank of participants;

This is the final article in our series about the pension plan, but information is always available, whether from your Information Booklet or benefits coordinator.

- Actuaries and consultants, who perform actuarial valuations at least every three years;
- T.A.L. Investment Counsel, which invests the pension fund in accordance with the investment policy determined by the pension committee;
- Royal Trust, which acts as fiduciary, where contributions are deposited by the divisions and issues pension cheques, as determined by the administrator;
- Samson Belair, auditors who prepare the financial statements.

Information

A personal statement showing accrued pension benefits, an estimation of the pension benefits for planning purposes (for those who work until the age of 65), contributions and accumulated interest, and an outlined summary of the main components of the pension plan are sent to all participants annually.

Regulations

Your pension plan is registered with Revenue Canada and the Quebec Pension Commission, and takes into consideration provincial regulations of the participants.

Every year, your T4 will indicate your pension adjustment, and Revenue Canada will inform you of the maximum contribution you can make to your Registered Savings Plan. *

What We Do
Putting the pieces together

When printed pieces come off the presses, the manufacturing process may be complete, but the job isn't necessarily ready for the customer.

That's where inserting comes into the picture. We add value to printed products by assembling them, so customers don't have to do it themselves.

In the Western Division, there are two methods of inserting. One is by hand, as it's done in Calgary, and one is by machine, as done in Miami Valley. We're taking a look at each of them in this issue of Inside News.

Miami Valley
At Miami Valley, inserting is done by a Kansa inserting machine.

Cathy Johnson, the Bindery Operator, says, "Our regular jobs include a monthly newspaper for the American Automobile Association, which can have some very original inserts. Another one, IGA, can have as many as seven inserts going into one book—some printed here, some outside the plant."

"A couple of inserts that were really interesting were a chair and a cellular phone. The chair was a recliner, in thick paper, with the feet up and the back reclining. The cell phone had an extended antenna, and was difficult to insert without tearing off the antenna," adds Cathy.

On the Kansa, the stations are lined up side by side. A jacket goes down the line, and is opened by suction, and inserts are place inside. At the stations, people have bundles of jackets and inserts, and feed them into the machine. Completed pieces go down the line and into a stacker, which makes bundles, which are then tied, and picked up by materials handlers.

> ...volume [in Calgary] ranges from 2.5 million to 4 million copies a week. All done by 78 inserters on 4 shifts, each with two very fast hands.

The machine can handle quantities from a single sheet to a 48 page insert, and anything up to thick cardboard. Capacity on a shift of 11-and-a-half hours has been as high as 186,000 completed pieces.

Stuff happens
The Kansa is very fast—and sensitive. Cathy notes, "The machine is picky about curled corners, and about dust on its sensors. When dust gets on the eyes, the machine shuts itself off, and an alarm bells rings. Then we have to go to the light panel to find the problem area, and clean the eyes."

"Static electricity can also be a problem," she adds. "It builds up when paper slides across the machine, and the weather outside makes a big difference. To ease the static, we use gas mineral spirits. Wet weather also increases the amount of paper curling."

Still, Cathy likes the Kansa, which she says is a lot cleaner and better than the old inserting machine it replaced.

Calgary
The Inserting department starts with job information, which it receives from Customer Service. That, in turn, leads to scheduling of jobs and inserters. Terryl Frederick, the Inserting Coordinator, says, "Most of our jobs are scheduled, but sometimes, we have surprise, short-notice jobs, because a customer's needs change or the presses can't run the product as expected, and we fill the gap."

The product arrives on skids at one of the two inserting tables. It comes in two parts: the carrier and the insert, with the carrier being the outside part and the insert going inside it.

Inserters stack carrier and insert bundles on their stands, and then put inserts into the carriers. After

Continued on Page 7

Inside News

The Transcontinental Western Regional Employee Newsletter

Editorial Board: Wayne Martyn, Neil LaRocque, Bob Abbott
Vancouver Editor – Marilyn Young – (604) 540-2333
Winnipeg Editor – Dave Craig – (204) 633-8890
Calgary Editor – Neil LaRocque – (403) 258-3788
Miami Valley Editor – John Meadows – (513) 879-5678

Calgary Quality Council
Faxletter

January 1995

Working Together

Teams and teamwork were the focus of the Information Session presented by the Calgary Quality Council on November 14, 1994.

Jim McPhail led a workshop that looked at four aspects of teams:
- Exploring how to harness the power of teams to improve customer satisfaction, cost, and cycle time.
- Assessing an organization's current situation with teams and where it needs to go.
- Examining the cultural and structural changes necessary to close the gap between the current situation and the desired situation.
- Gaining an understanding of what's involved in making these changes.

John Dempster made a presentation that looked at the roles of strategic and task teams. Strategic teams, he says, deal with policies, structure, and objectives. And, by dealing with them, the organization sets a foundation for transforming the style of management. In turn, transformed management will enable a company to capture its market.

Applying ISO 9000

At the Information Session on December 12, **Bernard Cook**, the Quality Assurance Manager at Travis Chemicals Inc., led a discussion about ISO 9000. The discussion followed a brief presentation by Mr. Cook, who explained the process involved in getting ready for registration. He also explained the auditing process and offered some tips on how to survive one.

Coming Up

Success Stories:
Public Sector/Private Sector

Quality Improvement in local government (City of Airdrie)

Technology company succeeds with Quality (ACTC Technologies Inc.)

- Find out what they achieved
- Learn how they did it
- Put their experience to work for you
- Ask them questions

Monday, January 9, 1995
7 p.m. to 9 p.m.
RGO Room, Scurfield Hall
University of Calgary
Fee: $5.00 for members, $10.00 for non-members (Memberships available at the door)

For more information, call the Council's answering machine at 286-0633 and leave a message.

Quality Management & Service

Bill Schnitzler, Coordinator - Continuous Quality Improvement, Energy Resources Conservation Board, speaks on Quality Management and Service.

Presented by: ASQC Calgary Section
Wednesday, January 18, 1995
Palliser Hotel
Refreshments at 5:30 p.m.
Dinner at 6:00 p.m.
Members: $23.00
Non-members: $25.00
To reserve, call xxx-xxxx

More Community Quality Councils?

The Quality Council of Alberta (QCA) is developing a program to encourage the rural communities of Alberta to adopt the principles of Total Quality Management. The format for doing this is to have them form Community Quality Councils (like the Calgary Quality Council), and to have these councils trained in the key aspects of selecting projects and teams, and managing the projects to a successful conclusion using a proven continuous improvement process.

The first step in this program was a QCA sponsored conference in March 1994. About 75 delegates from rural communities attended. It featured experts from the USA and Canada, who introduced delegates to the concept of community councils, and gave many examples of the successes that these councils were bringing to their communities. At the end of the conference, the delegates decided that the next step should be a working session for the interested people, on how to make it happen. Mount Royal College was asked to put it together.

In response, a workshop was held on November 30, 1994, co-sponsored by the QCA and Prosperity South, an organization promoting economic development. About 25 community leaders attended, and left with the feeling that they were on their way. The workshop featured success stories, including the accomplishments of the Calgary Quality Council, and addressed issues such as: creating a community vision, a community mission statement, and an action plan to make it happen.

The participants came away from the workshop enthused and ready to go to work in their local communities. We congratulate **Lloyd Rankin** and **Lorne Tetarenko**, who did an excellent job in leading the workshop.

Video Review
Unleashing the Power of Creativity: the Key to Teamwork, Empowerment, and Continuous Improvement

By: Ed Tickles

This 40 minute video provides a practical approach to creative problem solving, through the use of the "Advantages, Limitations, Unique Characteristics (ALU)" analysis method. The video uses good examples to help the viewer unleash the power of creative problem solving.

It also introduces the concept of the "Forced Relationship Technique." Throughout the video presentation, references and links are continually made to the overall Quality Management theme and process.

For more information, contact:
Kinetic Inc.
408 Dundas Street East
Toronto, Ontario M5A 2A5
Phone: 1-800-263-6910
Fax   1-416-925-4653

Want to Join In?

If you would like to take an active role in the affairs of the Calgary Quality Council, please let us know.

We currently need a couple of volunteers to help our Membership Team develop and deliver more member services, and we need two new Directors for the Board of Directors.

If either of these opportunities interest you, please call **Bob Abbott** at 948-7774 or leave a message at 286-0633. We look forward to hearing from you.

Section 1: Strategy

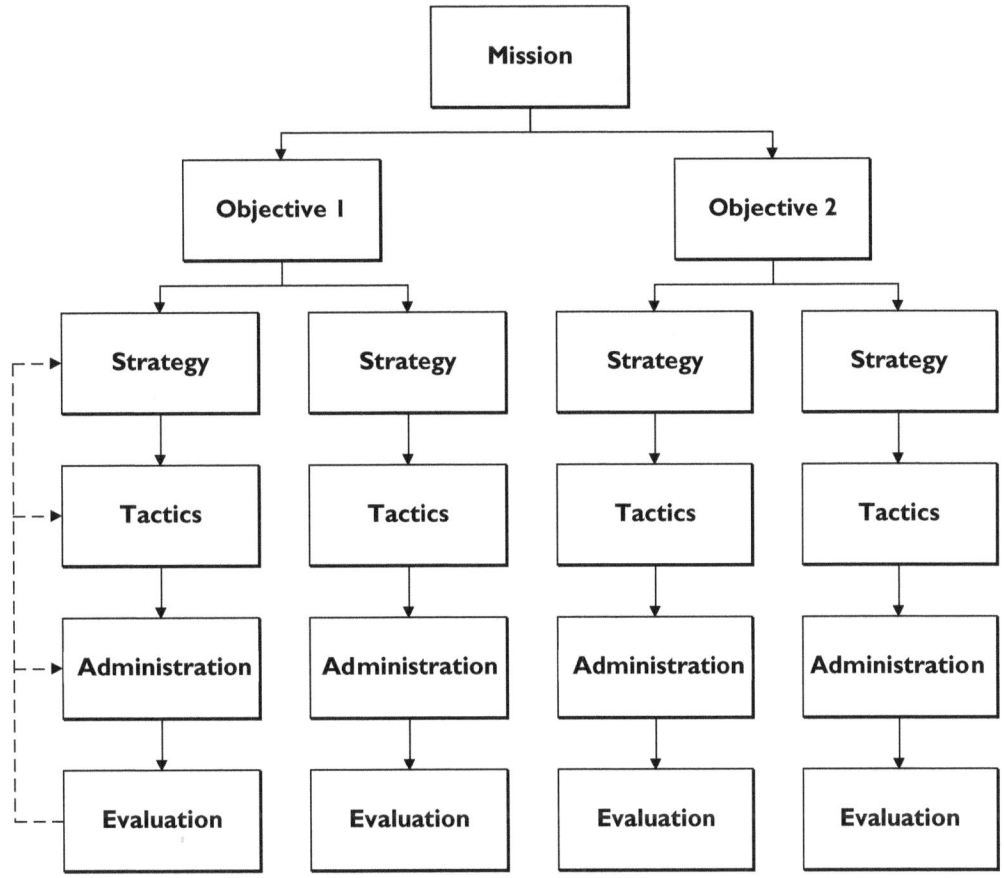

In this book, we think of strategy as a broad, overall plan that provides direction to managers, editors, journalists, and others responsible for key objectives. Of necessity, it is somewhat abstract (tactics provide the specific plans that make a strategy operational). In the case of a communication strategy, there are three essential components:

1. An organizational objective, expressed as reader actions
2. An identified group of readers who will act, and
3. A medium (whether a newsletter, print, or broadcast vehicle) through which readers will be sent messages about what action to take

In the *Strategy* section we discuss:
- *The medium:* Understanding newsletters and selecting a medium (Chapter 1)
- *Objectives:* Developing your objectives in terms of reader actions (Chapter 2)
- *Reader needs:* Getting and keeping reader attention (Chapter 3)

Chapter 1
Why newsletters? Why now?

In this chapter...

In this chapter, we deal with three fundamental questions. First, why would we use a mass medium for communicating? In most cases, the answer has to do with persuading stakeholders to think or act in a certain way. The mass media, including newsletters, are tools for persuasion.

Second, we ask why newsletters have become so popular within the spectrum of mass media. The answer to this question has two parts. First, new tools (particularly computers) made them feasible. Second, demand factors made them necessary. Demand factors include

- The expectations of stakeholders
- The splintering of mass audiences into smaller segments (or niches)
- The need for specialized communication vehicles for the discussion of complex issues
- The need among modern organizations to develop internal communication expertise
- The requirement that subject matter, timing, cost, and context be controlled

Third: Why a newsletter? In other words, why use a newsletter to communicate, and not some other method such as display advertising in a newspaper? This can be answered by noting that newsletters possess strong advantages when communication is driven or affected by one or more of the demand factors. Newsletters are not necessarily the only choice, but they are certainly an important option, now that supply factors have made them readily accessible.

Three questions

While the title of this chapter poses two questions, we actually deal with three – the two in the title and another implied by the first two:

1. Why would we want to use the mass media?
2. Why have newsletters become so popular in recent years?
3. Considering all the mass media vehicles that exist, why choose a newsletter?

Why mass media?

Modern organizations, whether for-profit or not-for-profit, whether big or small, form part of a web of dependence and interdependence. They cannot reach – or even move toward – their goals without the contributions of many people: those who join organizations and become members, those who buy products and become customers, those who join the company as employees, and so on. We refer to these people collectively as stakeholders.

But not every new member helps an organization meet its goals, and not every employee performs as the employer would like. Issue-driven advocacy associations can't take for granted that everyone affected by an issue will become a member or even voice support. Not every prospective customer makes a first purchase, and not every customer comes back to buy again. In short, organizations must compete for the attention, loyalty, and contributions of stakeholders or potential stakeholders. They must influence or persuade stakeholders to act or think in ways that contribute to the organizational goals.

The mass media satisfy the needs of modern businesses, associations, and other organizations for vehicles of persuasion. Newspapers, commercial radio and television broadcasts, and company newsletters exist to influence their readers, listeners, or viewers. A television station, for example, would like to persuade you to watch its evening news program rather than that of one of its competitors. And, if you watch its program, you see commercials aimed at persuading you to buy or do something. The programming comes at no nominal cost, but we know it won't remain available if commercials don't persuade us to become customers.

Even public broadcasting fits the persuasion category, although less directly. Public radio and television stations were created to promote certain kinds of cultural objectives and to influence society in various ways.

A closer look at persuasion

In her book *Persuasion in Practice* (1991), Kathleen Kelley Reardon writes, *"Persuasion involves guiding people toward the adoption of some behavior, belief, or attitude preferred by the persuader through reasoning or emotional appeals."*

It's a good definition, and we can learn a great deal by considering each section of it within a newsletter context. First, *Persuasion involves guiding people*. Persuasion isn't coercion or manipulation; it's an attempt to direct or influence people. Next, the word *adoption* means that only the person being guided can respond. The persuader – the publisher – can suggest, but only the person being persuaded – the reader – can adopt. This idea is captured by the old saying, "You can lead a horse to water, but you can't make it drink."

What we're trying to influence is a *behavior, belief, or attitude*. We'll deal with this idea in more detail later. Essentially it means that we want to affect the actions or thinking of the other person or persons.

The *preferred by the persuader* qualification recognizes that the communicator (the publisher) tries to influence the receiver (the reader), and that the communicator wants to convince the receiver of the superiority of another *behavior, belief, or attitude.*

Finally, persuasion means we try to influence others by making an appeal to their *reason or emotions*. Reason suggests some appeal to logic, while emotion suggests involuntary responses such as love, anger, sorrow, and fear.

In this book, we talk about influencing behaviors or attitudes by delivering those *reasoning or emotional appeals*. The vehicle for those appeals, of course, is the newsletter.

Why now?

No doubt you get quite a few newsletters, as I do. But, if asked what newsletters you receive, and when, you'd probably be hard pressed to provide details. After all, receiving a newsletter is no longer a novelty.

It hasn't always been that way. The free newsletter (also called non-subscription, advocacy, or stakeholder newsletter) has come into widespread use only recently, although it has been around for a long time. In this section, we examine some reasons for this newfound popularity, and in so doing, we set the stage for discussion of their strategic use.

This growth in popularity occurred because two important trends converged. New technology made this kind of publishing possible and widely accessible, through ease of use and lower costs. And at the same time, broader changes in society led to a need for narrowly targeted information vehicles.

We call these the *supply* and *demand* sides of newsletter publishing, as shown in Figure 1–1.

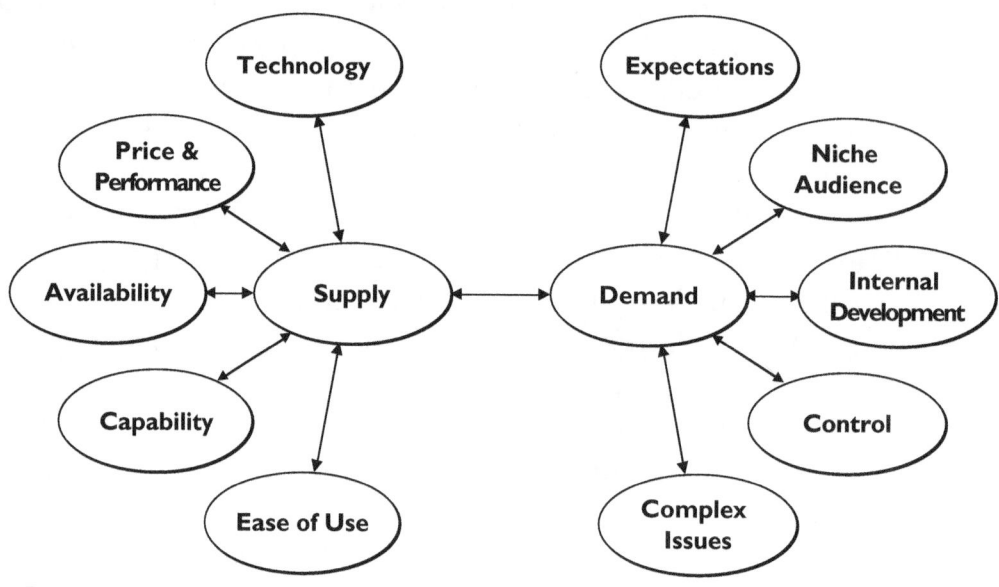

Figure 1–1

Let's look at each of the elements in more detail.

Supply

New and Better Tools

When we look at the supply side we mainly consider technology, especially the personal computer, as well as the software and peripheral hardware that support it.

Newsletters once were created with typewriters. This restricted the medium to truly dedicated communicators (not to mention dedicated readers), or to the subscription market. Imagine, if you will, counting the number of strokes you type on each line, and evening out (justifying) the right margin by manually dispersing blank spaces on each line. That represented just part of the labor-intensive effort. Cut and paste really did mean cut and paste, with scissors and glue. Wealthier organizations could send all that work to print shops, but however the job got done, a newsletter cost someone a lot of money or time.

Personal computers and word processors offered the first major advances, followed by desktop publishing software, including page layout programs. Now, publishers who weren't printers could keep more of their work in their offices and reduce their dependence on outside suppliers, as well as cutting the cost of using them. The laser printer added at least two important improvements: a more professional appearance for the end product, and the ability to print small runs internally. This march of technology continues, with online services, scanners, CD–ROMs, and other tools providing even more resources to organizations that do their own publishing. More recently, we've seen a profusion of electronic newsletters, which are distributed on computer networks, including the Internet.

Costs

Because of these changes, the cost of communicating with stakeholders dropped dramatically. Not only did overall costs go down, but the cost of reaching each reader dropped steadily, all of which made newsletters accessible to more and more organizations.

Costs figure in other ways, too. Newsletters offer organizations selective reach: the ability to send messages to narrowly targeted groups of readers. Mass media advertising, on the other hand, is not very selective: advertisers pay for both the audience they want and the audience they don't want. The same holds, to a lesser extent, for specialized and trade media.

Granted, newsletters still cost money. But with a newsletter, the sponsoring organization has greater latitude in spending. It can reduce costs by generating editorial matter differently, by using fewer colors, and through many other changes. Also, instead of having to make a buy or don't buy decision (as is often required for advertising), a company using a newsletter can adjust spending in small increments. This makes it possible to modify spending from period to period, or according to changing requirements.

Ease of Use

Ease of use also came with new technologies. As computers, software, and peripherals evolved, they became more user-oriented and sophisticated. In addition, the maturing of technology meant hardware and software companies began to emphasize ease of use as a competitive advantage. All of this broadened the user base, as well as the types and quantity of support (such as newsletter templates added to desktop publishing software, new how-to books, and better monitors).

Demand

We've also seen important changes that increased the demand for newsletters.

New Expectations

More and more stakeholders – whether customers, employees, members, or others – now expect to be informed, and even consulted, about events and processes that affect them.

This is no coincidence. Many organizations depend on the knowledge and skills of their stakeholders for success, because they use data, information, or knowledge to create value. Employees, for example, need to know much of what management knows, and that knowledge must be nurtured and stimulated constantly.

Niche Audiences

The splintering of previously large audiences into many smaller segments created narrow niche audiences for information. No longer can you count on your daily newspaper, or even industry publications, to provide enough relevant information about specific issues. Not only are there too many specialized issues for any single mass medium to track, but the expertise required to report on all of them is not available within any one organization. Both subscription and non-subscription newsletters can provide the kind of specialized reporting required, and in many cases it would not be available without them.

Complexity of Issues

The increasing complexity of issues and products also increased demand for newsletters. Technology, globalization, shifts in social structures, and other issues generated a need for new information forums, such as employee newsletters that explain the introduction of new management practices in the workplace, or marketing newsletters that update customers on the changing capabilities of sophisticated technical products.

Internal development

As the need for communication within and among organizations increased, so too did the need to train and develop communicators. By publishing newsletters, many organizations provide hands-on opportunities to learn about communication and to gain experience doing it. Even those not directly involved with the writing and publishing process may learn to communicate more effectively. Managers and employees, for example, may articulate their ideas more lucidly if someone from the internal newsletter asks them to explain what they're doing or why they're doing it.

Control

Organizations that want to control their exposure to the rest of the world also turn to newsletters. By using newsletters, they can control subject matter, timing, cost, and context.

The organization decides what gets published, who participates in a story, what aspect of the article receives emphasis, and who sees it. Timing means control over when the subject is raised, and when it gets withdrawn from discussion.

Context is important because it often has a strong effect on reception of the message. It can have two aspects. First, it can mean defining the framework within which a message is placed: for example, how returns on investments have been affected by the national economy. Second, it involves physical placement: proximity can suggest connections, and distance can suggest absence of connections among messages.

Newsletters allow sponsoring organizations to tell their stories in their own ways. They can position themselves with readers as they wish, address the issues that are important to them, stipulate who reads the messages, and decide how often readers will see their messages.

A note of caution: Our discussion may sound somewhat adversarial, as it compares newsletters with other media. But that shouldn't keep us from acknowledging the strengths of the other media. For some purposes, those vehicles will be more effective than newsletters.

Why a newsletter?

When it's time to decide whether or not to publish a newsletter, the decision should be based on the demand issues. The supply issues can be largely ignored.

You can ignore the supply side because it deals with enabling issues. The fact that we *can* publish a newsletter doesn't mean we *should*. And if we *should*, but don't have the expertise, it's readily available. For example, a person on staff can be sent to training, or freelance writers, editors, desktop publishers, and others can be contracted. Many of the tasks involved in publishing a newsletter are easily contracted out. And the enabling knowledge you need for planning and execution comes in this book.

On the other hand, if demand factors indicate that a newsletter is appropriate, then it does make sense to use one. As you'll recall, those factors include

- New expectations among stakeholders
- A niche audience

- Complex issues
- Internal development of staff
- Control

If one or more of those factors figures largely in your considerations, then a newsletter may be a practical solution to your communication needs.

For example...

Let's wrap up this chapter with a look at the reasons why the three organizations profiled in this book chose to communicate through newsletters. A copy of each of their newsletters can be found in the Introduction. First, here's an overview of the demand-side factors for each:

	TCP	**CQC**	**SG**
Expectations	✔	✔	✔
Complex Issues	✔		
Niche Audience	✔	✔	✔
Internal Development			
Control		✔	✔

TCP = Transcontinental Printing Inc.
CQC = Calgary Quality Council
SG = The Sovereign General Insurance Company

Employee newsletter: *Inside News*
Expectations

The employees of Transcontinental Printing are asked to make many changes in their work lives. New technologies and processes, an increasing emphasis on health and safety issues, shifting needs among customers, and other issues all combine to make their work increasingly complex. To cope with these changes, they need – and expect – information and direction.

Inside News helps serve these needs by providing articles that report on technological change, that indicate where the company is headed in the short and longer terms, and that illustrate how other employees in the division are changing and adapting.

Complex issues

The use of a newsletter also is appropriate because the company deals with many complex issues. The preparation of documents for the presses, for example, has gone from scissors, paste and T-squares to computers, electronic documents, and digital transmission in just a few years, and will continue to change through the foreseeable future.

The newsletter supplies new information and supplements information from other sources, especially by providing context. That is, it offers both the bigger picture and the hands-on experiences of peers within the company.

Niche audiences
The employees of Transcontinental's Western Division constitute a distinct, definable audience with common interests. Within this niche, we can further identify two subsets: one is within individual plants, and the other is inter-plant.

Indeed, inter-plant communication is becoming a source of competitive advantage, as new practices and techniques move from plant to plant at the employee level. *Inside News* helps with this form of communication, as the best practices move from plant to plant more quickly, with employees exchanging information.

Membership newsletter: *Calgary Quality Council Faxletter*
Expectations
One of the most important benefits of membership in any organization or association is the information members receive. Whether new techniques from a health association for lessening pain or new equipment news from trade associations, members expect helpful information.

For members and potential members of the Calgary Quality Council, the expectation of receiving relevant information was particularly important. Total Quality Management (TQM) and Quality Assurance (QA) were relatively new and complex management systems, demanding a great deal of information and knowledge.

Niche audience
The audience for TQM and QA represented a subset of people in managerial positions. That niche within management included managers with specific responsibility for Quality activities, as well as other managers and staff with an interest in promoting Quality initiatives within their organizations. The audience also included a significant number of consultants, trainers, and others who served Quality-specific needs of managers.

Control

In an ideal world, the Council and the organizations with which it cooperated would have had plans, venues, speakers, and other details arranged and confirmed well in advance. But, of course, that's not always possible, especially for organizations of volunteers who often make arrangements as they go. The CQC needed control over the timing of its communication, and a newsletter made that possible. That control was enhanced by the use of fax transmissions as the principle means of distribution. Changes could be made up until the moment the newsletter was distributed by fax.

Marketing newsletter: *The Sovereign Report*
Expectations

Insurers and brokers are bound together by their common need to take care of the brokers' customers, and by their need to compete with insuring organizations that use other channels. Because of this relationship, brokers expect insurers to advise them about issues that affect their business and their customers. (Brokers who represent The Sovereign also compete with each other to a certain extent, and with other brokers who use the same distribution channel, but that is of lesser importance for our discussion.)

Niche audience

Because The Sovereign deals with a limited number of brokers – about 10% of all brokers in Canada (a niche audience within the brokerage community) – a newsletter makes more sense than other forms of communication. Buying space in industry periodicals, for example, would not be as cost-efficient as a newsletter, since the company would pay for all of a periodical's readers, including brokers with whom it doesn't deal, employees and managers of other insurance companies, other industry players such as claims adjusters, and so on. As long as the costs of preparing, printing and distributing *The Sovereign Report* remain reasonable, it is more cost-effective than less targeted periodicals.

Control

By having its own newsletter, The Sovereign General can tailor the messages to its brokers specifically. In developing its messages, it does not concern itself with spillover into other segments of the brokerage community or the industry in general. In other words, it can discuss issues it would not discuss if it were communicating through industry periodicals.

Chapter 2
Your needs and objectives

In this chapter...

In this chapter we ask the second strategic question: "What do we want?" In other words, what are the objectives for the newsletter?

The process of setting objectives begins with knowledge of the organization's overall goals or mission. Newsletter objectives state the action required to move the organization toward fulfillment of that mission. They may or may not be quantified, and may or may not specify times or dates. However, if the newsletter objectives align with the organizational mission, then the newsletter can be described as strategic.

Objectives for a newsletter should be stated in terms of reader responses. In generic terms, the response involves either an attitude or a behavior, and either a change or reinforcement. Thus, four possible combinations exist:

- Reinforce a behavior
- Reinforce an attitude
- Change a behavior
- Change an attitude

These combinations cannot be your objectives in their own right. They can, however, help clarify what kind of response is desired.

Your newsletter may have more than one objective. Multiple objectives pose no problems as long as they are generally consistent with each other.

And even within a niche readership, expect a range of reader attitudes and behaviors across a spectrum, and set your objectives accordingly.

A strategic newsletter

As we pointed out in Chapter 1, anyone can publish a newsletter: the tools are now readily available. But a newsletter that effectively serves an organization demands more than just tools.

It requires a purpose, preferably an articulated purpose. For the organization as a whole, purpose may be captured by the mission statement, if one exists. Normally, the newsletter's purpose will be an extension of the organization's purpose or mission. For most newsletters, purpose is expressed through objectives. To some degree, at least, objectives answer the question, "What do we want?" This sense of purpose helps separate the strategic newsletter from its unfocused – and less productive – counterpart.

For example, a company's mission statement might call for a future in which it holds the largest market share among all firms in its industry. Its newsletter, in turn, might have objectives that call for it to generate new business and keep existing business. And when the newsletter objectives support those of the company, we can call the newsletter strategically positioned.

As we observed in the previous chapter, an organization achieves its ends or purposes by persuading stakeholders to act in its interests. The newsletter is a tool for persuading people to think or act in certain ways, and when the persuasion and the reader response align with the organizational purpose, the newsletter may be termed effective. In the terms of our earlier example, the generation of new business may be expressed as getting readers to call about a new product or service. The objective of keeping current business may be expressed as winning the trust of existing customers.

Figure 2–1 gives us a graphical overview of how purpose, objectives, the newsletter, and reader response all fit together:

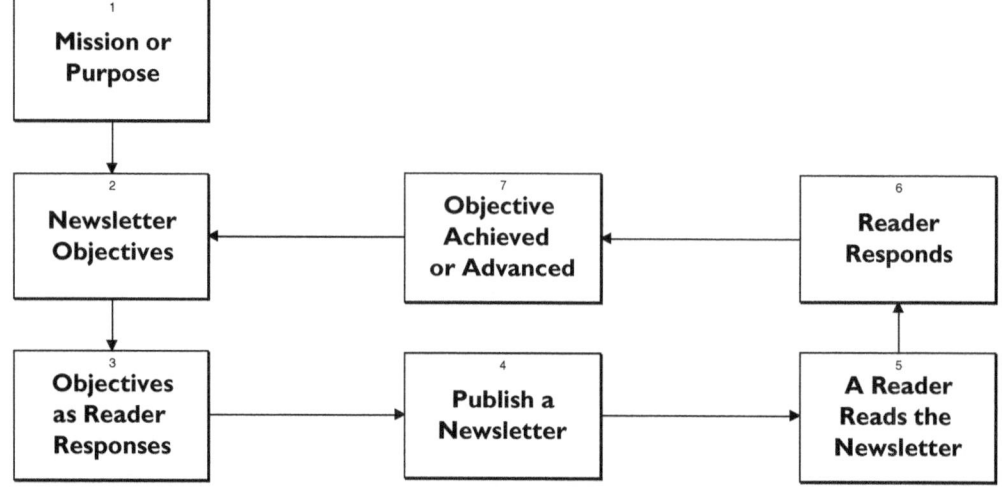

Figure 2–1

Considering this figure in more detail, and starting at the top, we see
1. The mission or purpose of the organization
2. Newsletter objectives
3. The objectives stated in terms of reader response — response to messages of persuasion.
4. Messages framed for the objectives are published in the newsletter
5. The reader receives the newsletter and reads it
6. After reading it, the reader acts or thinks in a particular way, as desired by the organization
7. When the reader responds, the organization achieves – or moves closer to achieving – its objective
8. (Step 2 repeated) The organization sets new or revised objectives for the newsletter, and the cycle starts over again

Note that the cycle restarts at Step 2, the newsletter objectives, rather than Step 1, the organizational purposes. That's because the mission of an organization remains relatively constant over time, while the objectives of individual departments or functions may change frequently.

In the following sections we deal with Steps 2 through 7 in more detail.

The nature of objectives (from Step 2)

While an organization's mission or purpose may be quite abstract, objectives tend to be more concrete or specific. They represent implementation of the mission. Objectives involve action: action directed toward ends.

Your objectives will at least specify the outcome you want, and may include actual numbers for those outcomes. That's up to you. While a set of numbers certainly provides benchmarks, quantities may not be practical in some cases. Until you've gathered data, you can't confidently make predictions. And if you use a newsletter for a purpose such as the promotion of a cause, it's unlikely that you will be able to gather data on exactly how many attitudes have changed, and by how much.

Putting a time dimension on an objective is also desirable, but again that depends on how accurately you can quantify the desired outcomes. And if you're working with attitudes, then time, like quantities, will be less essential.

So while you should include quantities and times if possible, they're not essential. What is essential, though, is the type of response desired. As we've argued, newsletters exist to influence or persuade readers to do something or think in a certain way. The response links the reader, whose actions or opinions help us reach our goals, and the goals themselves.

Reader response (from Steps 3 and 6)

Let's start our discussion of reader response with this proposition: If a newsletter exists to persuade, it can deal with either thoughts or actions. That takes in all possible human initiatives in a very broad way. We'll borrow a couple of terms from Reardon's definition, and call them attitudes and behaviors: attitudes to include all thought processes; behaviors to include all actions, which may or may not be preceded by thoughts. Everything else, such as intentions or beliefs, for example, can be considered a part of either attitude or behavior.

If there were any reason for doing so, we could subdivide our two categories into many component parts, but attitude and behavior neatly sum up what we need to know to create an effective newsletter.

When we work with attitudes and behaviors, we're involved in persuading. We may have either of two goals in mind: changing attitudes or behaviors, or reinforcing them.

Regardless of the type of newsletter, and regardless of whether it's printed, digitized for the Internet, videotaped, or on the radio, that's the full suite of choices. We can sum up the possible objectives, then, with the following four categories:

- Reinforce an attitude
- Change an attitude
- Reinforce a behavior
- Change a behavior

It helps to put the four categories into a matrix such as the one in Figure 2–2:

Change Attitudes	Reinforce Attitudes
Change Behaviors	Reinforce Behaviors

To use this matrix, simply ask yourself two questions: First, do you want to influence an attitude, or to influence a behavior? Second, do you want to reinforce it, or do you want to change it? Now, restate what you want readers to do as a result of reading your newsletter.

The four possibilities in the matrix cannot be objectives in themselves, but they do represent a way of categorizing the desired responses. One of the more difficult tasks faced by any manager responsible for a newsletter is the articulation of objectives so that others understand them. By thinking in terms of these four possibilities, we can sharpen our focus and provide a context that will help others understand our message.

Returning to our marketing newsletter example, we might say that we want to change the behavior of potential customers: we want them to stop buying from someone else, and start buying from us instead. So far as existing customers are concerned, we might state the objective as reinforcing their existing belief (the attitude) that our company provides the best value.

Publish a newsletter (from Step 4)

A decision to publish a newsletter should be based on the criteria listed in Chapter 1, under the heading of Demand Factors:
- The expectations of stakeholders
- The splintering of mass audiences into smaller segments (or niches)
- A need for specialized communication vehicles to discuss complex issues
- The need among modern organizations to develop internal communication expertise
- The requirement that subject matter, timing, cost, and context be controlled

Although we deal with some of these issues more extensively in other chapters, it may be helpful to review our objectives briefly in light of these demand factors, in the context of setting objectives.

Expectations among stakeholders: Are the responses you're seeking consistent with their expectations? For example, readers will expect a company that sells building supplies to try to influence their power tool purchases, but not their political beliefs.

Niche audiences: If you have quantified objectives, is the niche large enough to generate the quantities specified? Perhaps your persuasive marketing messages would be more effective if they were placed in magazines or newspapers.

Complex issues: If your message is relatively simple, perhaps some other medium could do the job as well or better. If your message is complex, is it so complex that it will diffuse reader response?

Internal development: Is there a tradeoff between developing employee skills, knowledge, or experience, and the response you expect from readers? For example, you might sacrifice some immediate reader response to give a talented but inexperienced writer a chance to work on the newsletter.

Control: Again, tradeoffs come to mind. If you ask an important client to write an article, you probably improve the odds of getting the desired response from readers. On the other hand, given the importance of the client, you may have to accommodate her schedule or style of presentation.

Readers (from Step 5)

This section relates mainly to marketing and sales newsletters, which have more discretion about selecting readers. For employee newsletters, obviously, targeted readers will be all employees, or all employees in a particular location or function. And membership newsletters normally go to all members, with perhaps a few to selected other organizations.

In the case of a marketing newsletter, selecting an audience takes more thought, because you have more discretion. Target too many readers or potential readers and you waste resources; target too few and you miss good prospects. We also must be concerned about the characteristics we use to define the audience: which ones really make a difference in terms of response?

Two common ways of segmenting potential readers are through demographic and psychographic analysis. We examine these types of analysis and others in more detail in Chapter 13. But, for the purpose of setting objectives, we'll provide a brief overview here.

Demographics refers to the so-called vital statistics: age, income, place of residence, education, and other non-subjective criteria. To set objectives, we want to know about the relationship between these characteristics and the nature of the desired response. For example, sending a newsletter about expensive cars to a low income neighborhood won't be very productive. In most cases, though, your marketing strategy already has built-in demographic characteristics or implications.

Psychographic analysis is less common. It draws distinctions among persons on the basis of criteria such as lifestyle and attitudes. More subjective than demographics, psychographics helps separate readers who might respond from those who might not. But creating or finding lists based on psychographics takes more time or money. In many cases, these lists come from surveys or from lists of respondents to earlier offers, or to offers from other organizations.

In this book, we use the word *readers* many times. In almost every case, you can assume that the word *targeted* precedes it. And your targeted readers (created by segmenting) are generally the same population as your niche audience or niche readership. We needn't dwell on these word definitions, though. We discuss them only to emphasize that newsletters work best when distributed to selected readers – those most likely to help you reach your objectives.

Objective achieved or advanced (from Step 7)

If readers respond as we wish, then we have achieved our objective, or at least advanced toward it. That also depends, of course, on how finely we specify our objective. If we include quantities and times, then we can clearly achieve or not achieve it. On the other hand, a non-specific objective cannot, by definition, be achieved. It can only be advanced.

It is important to recognize we can't take advancement for granted. The mere fact that we publish doesn't necessarily mean anything will happen. In light of our objective-setting exercise, we know that we have to be realistic, and assume nothing on the part of readers.

If you don't have any data or experience on which to base your numerical objectives, for example, then they won't mean much. If you haven't published a newsletter before, then you can't gauge with certainty, in advance, the effect it will have on readers.

Still, assuming you've seen results that are at least encouraging, then it's time to set new objectives. Or if the results don't meet expectations, then the existing objectives will have to be revised, or perhaps you'll drop the newsletter and use other media. A detailed evaluation process outlined in Chapter 15 helps troubleshoot or make decisions if your newsletter fails to generate reader responses.

The process

Setting newsletter objectives, then, involves at least two basic steps. First, we must identify the goals that the newsletter is to help accomplish. And second, we must identify what readers can do to help us reach or move toward those goals. Along the way, we're likely to take some side steps and intermediate steps, but these are the two key steps involved in setting effective newsletter objectives.

If you're like most of us, you'll end up with multiple objectives; sometimes because you want a number of responses from your target audience. Other times you'll have more than one objective because of the nature of your target audience. Having multiple objectives is not a problem, as long as they are reasonably consistent with each other.

Another common challenge, in addition to multiple objectives, is dealing with a range of reader attitudes and behaviors. While the audience may be targeted, any set of readers large enough to be meaningful to the publisher is sure to be diverse. Sometimes that requires restating the message in different ways, offering different incentives, or publishing separate editions. It sometimes requires publishing to the lowest common denominator.

Then again, a newsletter can take a two-step communication strategy. This means giving information to influential persons or leaders and letting them take the message to the rank and file. In this case, we see a double persuasion process: first the publisher persuades an opinion leader to respond, and then the leader persuades others to respond.

But...

Many publishers and would-be publishers of newsletters resist the idea that newsletters should persuade their readers of something. Instead, they say, "We just want to communicate with our members (or employees, or customers)." What that leaves unstated, of course, is the motivation for communicating. Can you responsibly commit time and money to a newsletter without some reason for doing so?

And the desire to achieve something through someone else motivates most communication. Even non-profit associations, prolific users of newsletters, want their members to renew or participate in some way. Communication almost always has a self-serving element.

I think, in fact, there always should be some conscious, self-serving reason for an organization to put time and money into a newsletter.

For example...

Now, let's look at the application of objectives in three actual newsletters.

Membership newsletter: *Calgary Quality Council*

The mission of the Calgary Quality Council was to champion the ideas of Quality (Total Quality Management and Quality Assurance). As a non-profit, advocacy organization the Council wanted to expand the use of these ideas within other organizations and the community, as well as act as a clearinghouse for information about Quality. To pursue and finance these objectives, it sold memberships and presented various learning and networking opportunities.

The Council's newsletter had multiple objectives arising out of this multi-pronged mission. It wanted readers to respond in several different ways:

- Adopt or maintain the principles of Quality (reinforce the behavior of some readers, change the behavior of others)

- Be advocates of Quality within their organizations and within the community at large (change the behavior of others)
- Attend presentations put on by the Council and other organizations with similar mandates (reinforce the behavior of some readers, change the behavior of others)
- Retain membership, or become members of the Council (reinforce the behavior of existing members, change the behavior of non-members)

Some readers had already adopted Quality and the Council wanted to reinforce their attitudes and behaviors. Others were still learning about this approach to management, and were being urged to change their attitudes and behaviors (in other words, to manage differently by using Quality).

You'll notice that the second objective (Be advocates of Quality within their organizations and the community at large) involved a two-step strategy. Readers of the newsletter were assumed to be opinion leaders who would change the attitudes and behaviors of others within their circles of influence.

Marketing newsletter: *The Sovereign Report*

The objective of *The Sovereign Report* is to maintain a strong relationship with brokers by transmitting a sense of The Sovereign General's corporate character and business philosophy. At the same time, though, it doesn't want to mail out what brokers would consider a blatant brochure.

Publication of the newsletter began after a company survey showed brokers wanted to know about the company, its philosophy, its intentions, and its opinions on the issues of the day. But instead of writing, "This is what we do; this is what we think," the company has tried to express its personality through its choice and treatment of subject matter.

More specifically, *The Sovereign Report* focuses on two types of articles: information articles about new or developing ideas for marketing, and articles on tactics and strategies for managing a business effectively.

The reasoning behind the first type of feature will be self-evident: Both The Sovereign General and brokers have a vested interest in the brokers' ongoing success. The rationale for the second is more complex. The company and brokers operate in a crowded, highly competitive market, and their business is cyclical with significant highs and lows of revenue and profitability. Effective management is critical: Any insurer or broker unable to manage effectively will be swept out of business during the lows in the cycle.

Because most, if not all, of these brokerages already manage well, The Sovereign's newsletter objective might be restated as reinforcing existing behavior. It encourages and helps brokers to continue marketing and managing effectively.

Employee newsletter: *Inside News*

Changes – in technology, customer needs, new management practices, and regulatory demands (such as environmental rules) – have had a major impact on the printing industry. Not surprisingly, the employees of Transcontinental want their newsletter to help them understand and deal with these issues, because their futures are tied to the future of the company.

You'll note we just wrote the *employees…want*, and not *management wants*. In this case, management pays for the newsletter, but content decisions are based on surveys of reader preferences, as well as other input from employees (and, to a lesser extent, from management).

On the surface, this puts *Inside News* outside the model we've developed, involving change or reinforcement of attitudes or behaviors. After all, the employees of TCP wouldn't be expected to persuade themselves of something. But, in fact, employees recognize that their work world is changing, and that their futures will be more secure if they understand it and adapt to it. So, we might consider the objective of *Inside News* to be a change in behavior, in this case the employees' own behavior, on the job.

This leads to the issue of reader diversity, the range of behaviors and attitudes that exists within a group of targeted readers. Attitudes and behaviors can't be classified as simple *either-or* characteristics. Instead, they need to be considered as a spectrum. For example, some employees will be enthusiastic about a change, and urge its immediate adoption. Others will resist the change as long as possible, and only adopt it when they have no other choice. In most cases of this kind, of course, the majority fits somewhere between the two extremes, with the greatest number clustered around the mid-point. And all of this means that *Inside News* sometimes deals with both reinforcement and change at the same time.

Chapter 3
Meeting reader needs

In this chapter...

Articulating what we want readers to do, as we did in Chapter 2, doesn't complete the job of framing an effective newsletter strategy. We also must determine what readers need or want from us.

Readers have goals, objectives, and dreams, as well as needs. But to achieve those desired targets, they must act, and that presupposes making choices about alternative courses of action. To help make those choices, they turn to many information sources, including newsletters. Normally, the making of choices is a process, one which we can model to illustrate the typical steps.

Choice-making processes don't operate in a vacuum, of course. So, if a publisher's strategy is appropriate, its sales, employee relations, or member relations process will intersect with the reader's choice-making processes. If they intersect or converge, then both reader and publisher will have gained something from the newsletter: the reader by getting information that helps him make his choices, and the publisher by having an opportunity to influence the choices made by the reader.

This means the publisher should not try to decide what's best for the readers, but should try to understand the needs of the readers, and serve them. And that takes us to another critical point: The publisher must be willing to provide what the reader wants or needs, and must be able to deliver: a newsletter is a major commitment for the publisher.

Goals, choices, and alternative courses

What we've seen in the first two chapters would suggest a one-sided relationship, with all the benefits on the publisher's side. But that would be a hasty conclusion.

Consider the newsletters you receive. Some of them you throw out without reading, and some you scan very quickly and then throw away – but others you make a point of reading carefully, because they contain something of interest or value to you. Perhaps you've been thinking about buying a bicycle, and a newsletter with information about trends in bicycle usage arrives. If you read this newsletter, you're being perfectly rational – and doing what the publisher hoped you would do.

That's because people, like organizations, have objectives and goals; but unlike organizations, people even have dreams. Our objectives, needs, or dreams may be personal, they may be vicarious – on behalf of another person – or they may be organizational: "I'm proud of my company!" While all of these are possible, we'll focus on personal needs for the sake of simplicity.

To satisfy our needs, we must act: We must belong, we must buy, we must do. And in doing and belonging and buying we must make choices. Making choices, especially important choices, presupposes the examination of alternative thoughts or actions.

The newsletter alternative

One source of information that helps us assess those alternative courses is the non-subscription newsletter. Sometimes readers already know what they want, and they use a newsletter as a source of information, whether for comparison purposes or for greater depth.

On the other hand, newsletters also can trigger awareness, letting readers know about opportunities to move closer to one or more of their goals. A marketing newsletter, for example, might lead a reader to see that the publisher's product would reduce the time spent doing a task, and as a result she would have more time to do something else of importance.

All in all, making choices involves many complex processes. But we can provide a generalized model, as shown in Figure 3–1: one that covers most choice decisions. It's an eight-step model that begins with awareness of a problem or opportunity:

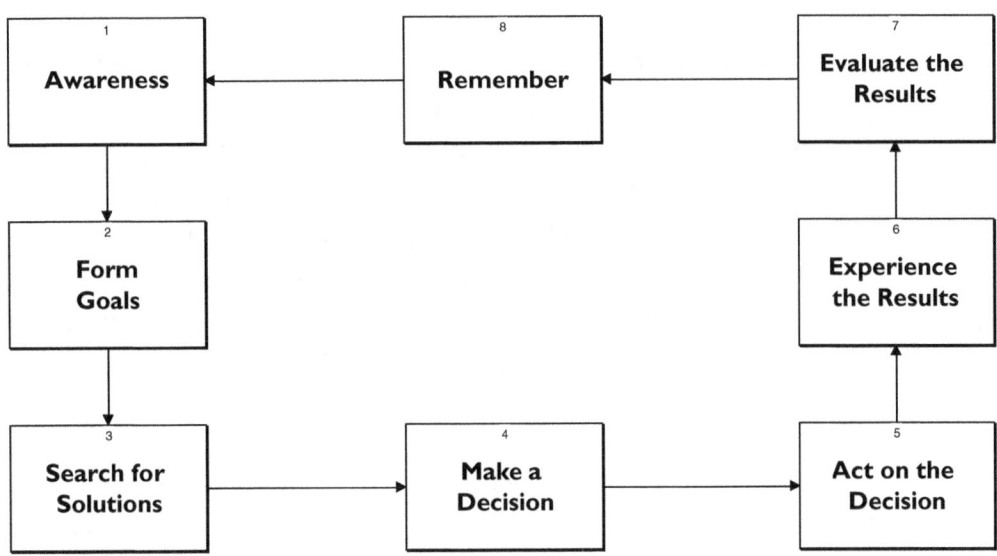

Figure 3–1

Here's an example that might be used in connection with a marketing newsletter:

1. *Develop awareness* of a problem or opportunity. Awareness occurs in the mind of the reader. It may be occurring now – "My car has broken down on the way to work again, and I need a new one." – or something that might happen in the future – "My car is making funny noises; I hope it doesn't cost a lot to fix." Whether this is a negative or a positive situation, a problem or an opportunity, the person knows he can or should do something.

2. *Form goals,* whether vague or specific – "I want to drive to work without worrying about breakdowns." These goals refer to a future state the person hopes to achieve or avoid, after becoming aware of the problem or opportunity. We might call them objectives, rather than goals, but we'll use the latter term. We distinguish goals of the reader from objectives of the publisher.

3. *Start a search* – take the next step: examine different ways to achieve the goal – "I could buy another car, or I could borrow John's." This search is likely to produce a set of alternative behaviors, but not necessarily a complete set. The comprehensiveness of the set usually reflects the importance of the problem. At this search stage, a newsletter becomes useful because it enables the reader to explore the alternative behaviors or thoughts that will help him achieve the goal.

4. *Make a decision* – select what appears to the best of the alternative solutions. Sometimes the person optimizes, aiming for the best solution. At other times, he may select one that's good enough, or opt for the

least unsatisfactory – "At least if I buy a car with fewer miles on it, it shouldn't cost as much to maintain."
5. *Act on the decision* – implement the selected alternative, which in this case means buying a car. This is the phase of the experience when the person acts. And when he responds, the newsletter publisher benefits, or at least has a chance to benefit. If the publisher is a car dealer, and the reader bought his car from that dealer's lot, then the dealer benefited. If the reader bought from another dealer, then the benefit is less tangible – the dealer had an opportunity to sell the reader a car, but didn't – but it's still a benefit.
6. *Experience the results* – "It sure is nice not to worry about my car breaking down." At this point the person starts updating his attitudes. Note, though, that this stage is distinct from evaluation, which comes next. This stage involves the reader's immediate reaction, not the comparison with what might have been.
7. *Evaluate the experience.* Now the experience is assessed in terms of the goals set earlier, or in terms of other alternatives that had been considered earlier. It also may involve an appraisal of the process – "I'll check out more dealers next time."
8. *Remember the evaluation.* By storing the evaluation in memory, the person saves information that will be useful when a situation like this comes up again. This memory forms part of an ongoing set of ideas and rules about this issue – in this case, buying a car.

Our model shows the process as being a loop or cycle, rather than a linear progression. That's because our experiences compound, which is to say we learn a bit more each time we go through them. So when we buy a car for the second time or the twelfth time, we bring to the process the experience and knowledge gained in previous searches and purchases.

This model also helps explain why most of us do read newsletters; at least good newsletters. While the model showed just one decision-making process, our lives are filled with them, from the mundane (what to eat for breakfast) to the profound (whether or not to make a lifelong commitment to a person or institution). At any given time, many of these decision processes go on simultaneously, and any information that helps us make these choices helps satisfy our needs.

Getting together

Now, let's look at a hypothetical case in which the needs of the reader and the publisher intersect. It illustrates what I call the unique, symbiotic relationship between publisher and readers.

Let's turn again to the example of the person whose car has broken down on the way to work. Follow the process that occurs by matching the numbers on the paragraphs with the numbers in Figure 3–2. And as you work through this figure, you'll note that it combines the newsletter loop shown in the previous chapter (Figure 2–1) and the decision model shown earlier in this chapter (Figure 3–1).

As the legend underneath the figure indicates, ovals refer to reader behaviors and thoughts (independently of the publisher); rectangles refer to the actions of the publishing organization; and rectangles with rounded corners refer to reader actions that affect the publisher.

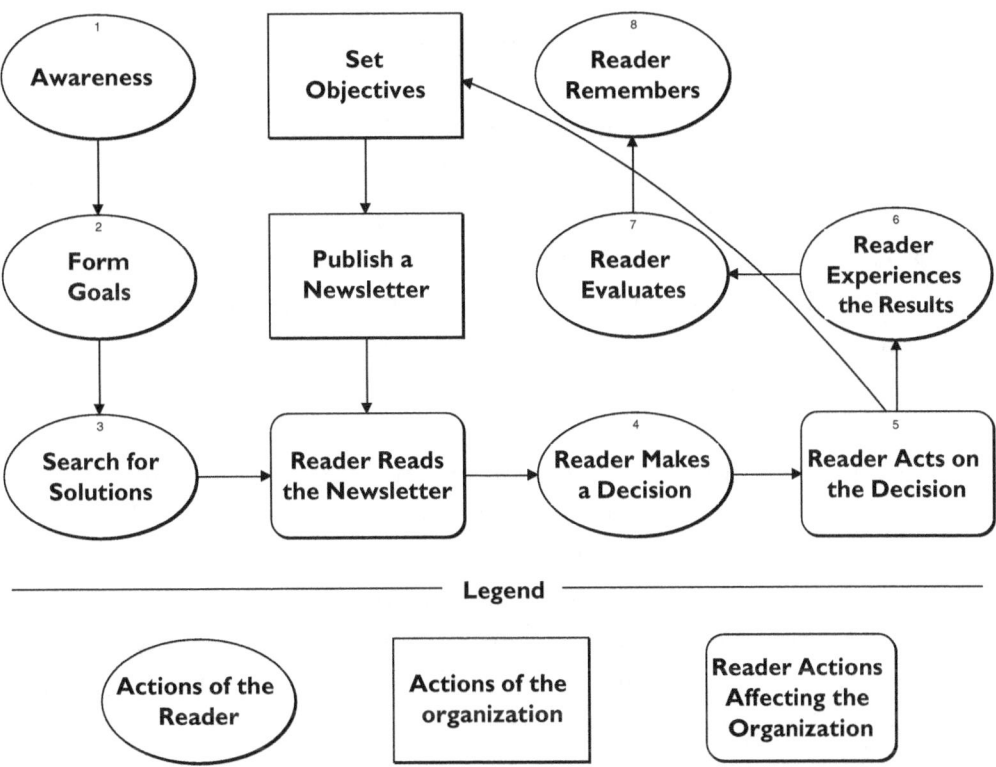

Figure 3–2

1. A man became aware of a problem when his car broke down. In this case, awareness was not triggered by reading a newsletter, but by circumstances in the reader's life. At about the same time, the car dealership published a newsletter, but of course, without knowing the intentions of this person. However, the dealer does know that a cer-

tain proportion of those within this target audience is likely to buy a car this month.
2. Our potential reader considers reliability very important, so he plans to buy a new car, reducing the risk of a break down. He forms *a goal*.
3. He has started thinking about the type of car that will suit him best. He starts to *search*. During this search, he receives a newsletter in the mail from the dealer, and because he's especially interested in this subject at this time, he *reads* it.
4. Articles in the newsletter talk about car warranties and roadside service, which he considers valuable, considering the breakdowns he's had recently. This, plus a visit to the dealership, leads him to *decide* that he will buy from this dealer.
5. Next, he signs a contract to buy the car: he *acts*.
6. After taking delivery of it, he notes how well it performs. He *experiences* the results.
7. He compares that performance to his expectations and original objective. This is the *evaluation*.
8. Finally, the reader establishes in his own mind the degree of satisfaction the car has brought him. He stores the evaluation in his *memory*.

While obviously simplified, our example does illustrate how both reader and publisher achieved their objectives by serving each other's needs. The newsletter provided information that the reader found helpful in searching for and selecting a new car. The reader helped the dealership (the publisher) achieve its objective of selling a certain number of cars in a specified period.

A similar set of dynamics exists between employees (readers) and their employers (publishers). Consider an article about health benefits in the newsletter. The newsletter explains to readers what their plan covers and how to make claims correctly, so that they're processed quickly. The employees gain by getting information that ensures that they don't miss any refunds to which they're entitled. The employer gains because fewer employees make demands on the benefits administrator's time with their questions about eligibility and claims procedures.

"Just say 'No'?"

When we discover what our targeted readers need or want, we should start serving that need. But there may be a temptation to say "No," to suggest that what readers want is inappropriate or wrong, and that they should be given something else, something we think it more important for them to consider.

We may be tempted to tell readers what we think they need, rather than what they've told us in surveys, focus groups, or other opinion-gathering exercises.

It's not hard to imagine the publisher of an employee newsletter arguing that employees need reminders about the need to work harder, not more information about trends in the industry. But if employees tell you that it's more important – to them – to know more about trends in the industry, then that's what you should give them. If you don't, then they may not even pick up the newsletter, let alone read it. And as we argue in this book, a newsletter that doesn't get read cannot influence the reader.

And more words of caution

When we attempt to deal with reader needs, we move into a new realm: one in which we don't have the same knowledge about needs and goals as we do about our own. Often, publishers deal with this situation by projecting their own views and preferences onto readers. In the case of an editorial board, the projections of several board members may compete, and ultimately they may arrive at some sort of compromise: one that reflects the views of the most insistent members. Neither approach does much for readers, whose views may or may not be reflected.

This can be dealt with in a number of ways. Perhaps the best way is through readership research, but that's not always possible. Alternatively, you can consider focus groups, reader surveys, and various segmentation strategies (for more on segmentation, see Chapter 13).

Regardless of how we approach reader needs, some care must be taken to ensure that they really are the needs of readers, and not our own.

A definition of non-subscription newsletters

Based on what we read in earlier chapters, we might have thought of the non-subscription newsletter as a tool of persuasion for the publisher.

But now that we better understand reader needs, we'll propose a new definition. *An effective non-subscription newsletter is a bargain between publisher and reader: The publisher provides free and useful information to readers, and readers open themselves to the publisher's attempts to influence the ways they satisfy their needs.*

And, a strategic newsletter is one in which the information provided aligns with both the objectives of the publishing organization and the needs of targeted readers (we'll discuss this type of content more extensively in Chapter 5).

Responding to persuasion

Readers probably don't make a conscious decision to open themselves to our persuasion. But they do understand the bargain, because they experience it every day as they listen to radio or watch television. Private broadcasters provide free content (whether music, news, drama, sports, or other programming), and in return, listeners and viewers willingly expose themselves to the commercials. Newsletters use the same model.

As an additional point of interest, the same model has become established, and popular, on the Internet. There are now literally tens of thousands of different newsletters, or e-zines (short for electronic magazines) available by e-mail. At the same time, sites on the World Wide Web have embraced the idea of giving away something of value, with the expectation visitors will end up buying from them or supporting their cause.

A critical point underlies this discussion: We must be prepared to determine what information readers want, and deliver it.

Demands on publishers

Willingness

If your organization has a secretive culture, one in which no one volunteers any significant information, then you probably should not have a newsletter. Some organizations find it very difficult to share knowledge and ideas, fearing that competitors will read the newsletter, that employees will take advantage of the information they receive, or that members might expect too much for their membership dues. Or they might be afraid that regulatory agencies will misconstrue their comments. Such fears may be legitimate, or may not. But as long as they exist a newsletter will not be effective, because it filters too finely the information that goes to readers.

Ability

Are you able to provide useful information to readers? Often, the people responsible for a newsletter get too busy doing other things to give much attention to the subjects that readers consider important. Perhaps the person who will write about a subject knows it well, but doesn't have or take the time to explain it to others with a less thorough understanding.

Will adequate resources be available to do the necessary research and development of articles? Can you afford the graphics that will help readers understand a complex subject? Our list could go on, but it should be clear that you need to be willing and able to provide information that is useful to the reader.

Commitment

If you make a decision to use a newsletter, then you must make a commitment to do it well, because readers will expect and demand it. In addition, a newsletter is not a one-time tool: It must be published regularly and over an extended period, to have a significant effect.

For example...

Marketing newsletter: *The Sovereign Report*

The insurance brokers who read this newsletter compete in a mature industry, one characterized by extensive channel competition (such as independent brokers vs. direct marketing insurers), and by price competition within their channel. Further, they function in a cyclical industry, with prices and margins fluctuating as capital moves in and out. Capital ebbs and flows according to the profitability of the financial services sector.

With these challenges, brokers take an interest in subjects related to marketing and to general management. These don't have to be insurance-based articles, since good marketers will use examples from other industries or sectors to find new competitive advantages. The same holds true for general management – managers take a strong interest in the management of insurance agencies, but readily recognize that good ideas can come from any sector. So, although the articles in *The Sovereign Report* don't necessarily deal with the insurance industry, they do address the needs of its readers. Annual surveys of brokers generate high approval ratings for the newsletter.

Employee newsletter: *Inside News*

Employees of the Western Region of Transcontinental Printing have a wide range of needs and objectives. Among the most widely represented are a desire for reassurance about job security (which is linked to the security of the company) and the need for information about benefits, changing technology, and effective job performance.

Take employee benefits, for example. Most employees want the financial protection offered by health, dental and pension plans. This subject consistently rates highly in reader preferences surveys. *Inside News* addresses that need by providing articles that explain the scope of benefits, when they take effect, and how to apply for them.

Benefits are an important interest of employees, but not their only interest. They also want to know about corporate plans and direction, customers, competitors, workplace practices, new technology, and trends in the industry. Information about these subjects helps them project their futures, and hold the course, or adapt, as necessary. As we'll see in Chapter 5, there is powerful convergence between the needs of employees and the needs of the organization that employs them.

In annual reader surveys, employees of TCP show a strong interest in articles and other content that help them understand and respond to needs they share with the company.

Membership newsletter: *Calgary Quality Council Faxletter*

Readers of the *Faxletter* shared a common interest, the Quality movement, whether that involved Total Quality Management or Quality Assurance. Every person who became a member of the Council or asked to be on its mailing list had a vested interest in the subject. In some cases, these men and women were responsible for implementing Quality initiatives in their organizations, and in other cases they championed the idea of Quality within their organizations, hoping to have it adopted by senior management.

As a result, they needed information and knowledge that would support their advocacy. The *Faxletter* provided that information to them in several ways. First, it provided notes about new sources of information, such as books and videos. Second, it offered advance notice of relevant coming events, both by the Council and other organizations. And third, it kept members informed about the direction and activities of the Council itself (the existence of the Council meant a source of information continued to be available to them).

Section 2: Tactics

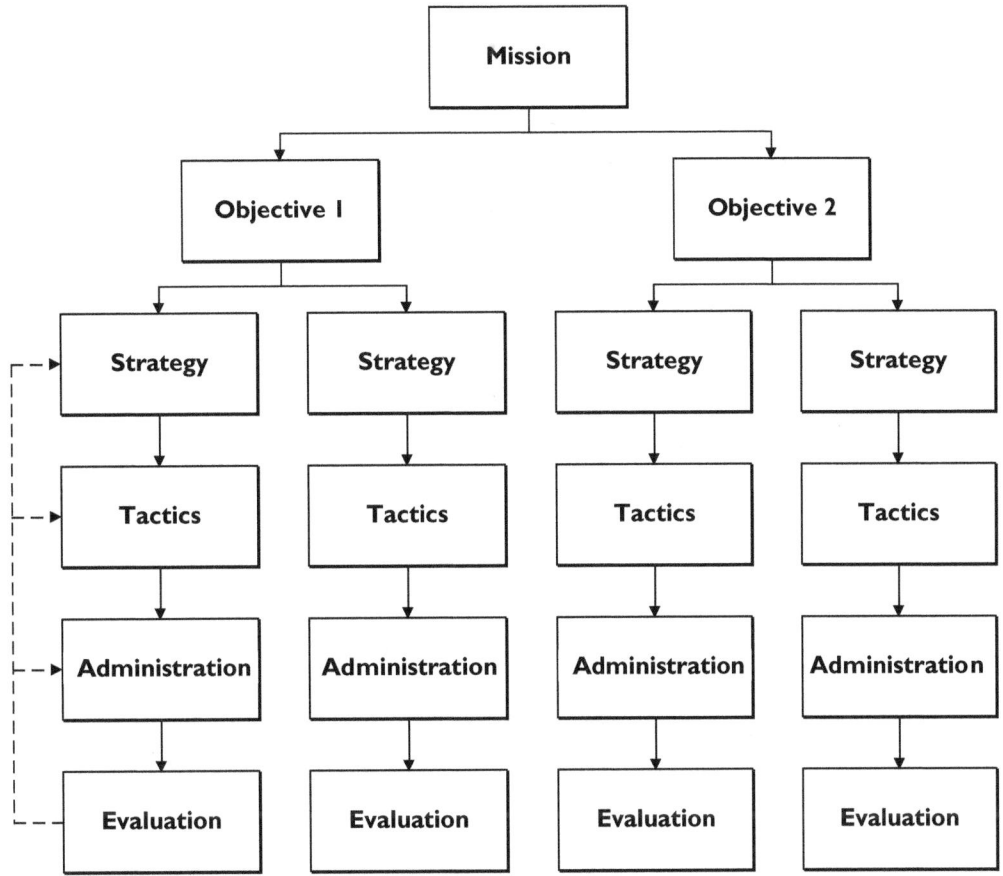

Earlier, we defined strategy as an overall plan or course of action—an abstract concept. Tactics, while still part of the planning process, are detailed and concrete applications of the strategy. They flesh out the strategy, and make the relationships among the objectives, medium, and audience more specific.

For newsletters, we work with four essential tactics:
- *Content:* Selecting subject matter (Chapter 5)
- *Presentation:* How the content is presented (Chapter 6)
- *Frequency:* How often to publish (Chapter 7), and
- *Size:* The number of pages (Chapter 7)

But first, in Chapter 4, we deal with two critical issues that underlie all tactical decisions, the willingness and ability of readers to read our newsletter.

Chapter 4
Willing and able readers?

In this chapter...

So far, we have taken it for granted that readers will read our newsletter and understand what's in it – but no longer. In this chapter, we deal with the issue by discussing two critical reader characteristics: Willingness and Ability. In doing so, we set a foundation for the tactics involved in newsletter publishing.

Willingness refers to the motivation of readers, and reflects several characteristics of the newsletter and the reader:

- Relevance of the content
- Credibility of the newsletter's sources
- The degree of reader involvement (also called interactivity)
- Emotions that readers bring to the newsletter
- Consistency of published views with existing reader views

Ability refers to the proficiency of the reader at understanding the words in the newsletter, as well as the messages in those words and the graphics. Issues affecting ability include

- Reading competence and readability
- Availability of context
- Level of abstraction in the wording and symbols
- Structure of text, graphics, and design

Willingness and ability are critical barriers. The reader must clear both, to get value from the newsletter for her own ends, or to respond to the publisher's messages.

An important *if*

Up to this point, we've assumed that if we publish a newsletter, readers will pick it up, read what we have to say, and act or think accordingly. Of course, that doesn't necessarily happen; they don't always read what publishers want them to read. And if they don't read the content, their attitudes or behaviors won't be influenced, and the newsletter effort will have been wasted.

Looking again at the basic newsletter loop (Figure 4–1, below), we see that there should be a decision point between the fourth and fifth elements.

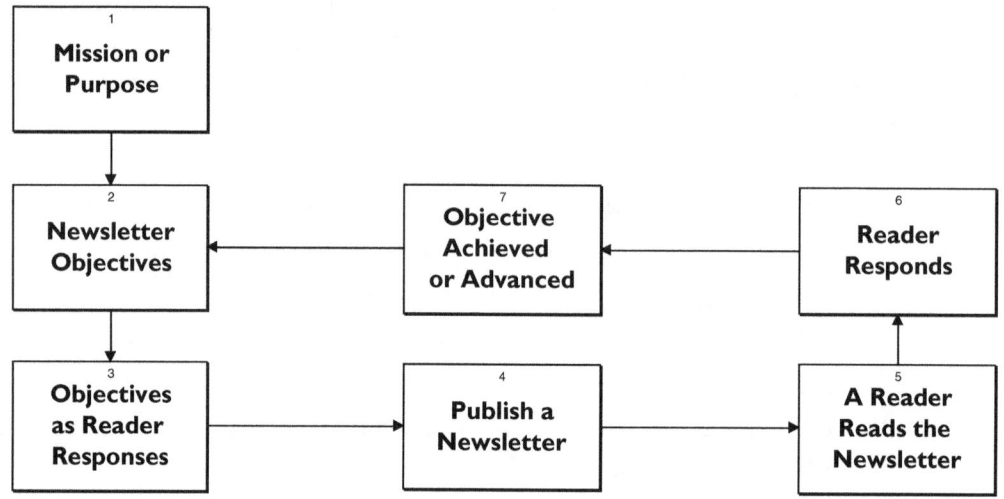

Figure 4–1

Instead of going directly from *Publish a Newsletter* to *A Reader Reads the Newsletter*, as the Figure 4–1 indicates, we ought to insert an important qualification: *If* the reader reads the newsletter. In other words, we distinguish between a member of the target audience receiving a newsletter and that individual reading it.

Only the reader can decide if she will or will not read the newsletter. Let's elaborate by adding this important question to the basic newsletter loop, as shown in Figure 4–2:

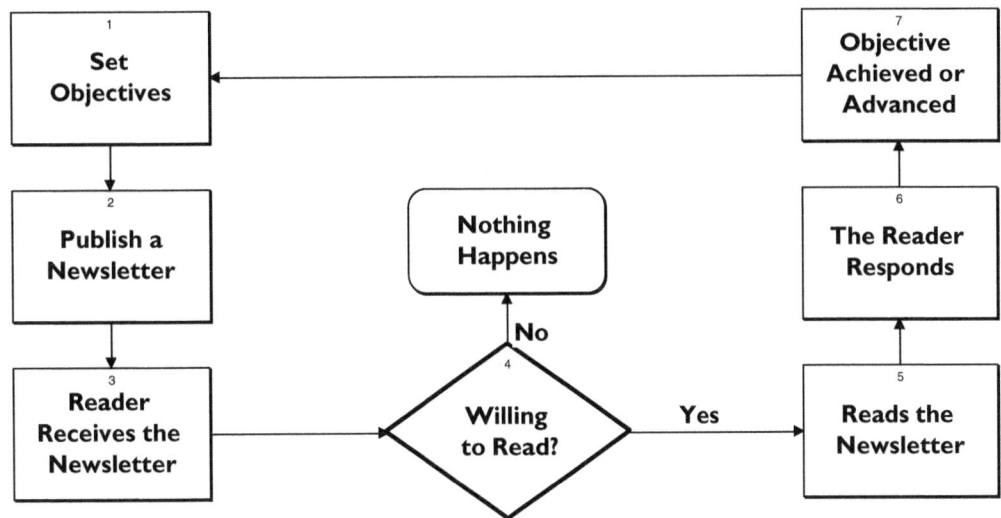

Figure 4–2

Willingness examined

Willingness is a complex issue, but by considering it within the relatively narrow confines of newsletter publishing, we can narrow it down to a manageable number of common dimensions:

- Relevance
- Credibility
- Involvement
- Emotion
- Consistency

While some dimensions may figure more prominently than others, no one of them, by itself, provides a full explanation of willingness. In most cases, several of them are important, both individually and in combination with each other. This will become clearer as we examine each one in more detail.

Relevance

For most readers, relevance tops the priorities. As we explained in Chapter 3, they want information that helps them reach their goals. And, without seeing some apparent connection to their goals, readers see no benefit in investing time in the newsletter. There are exceptions, of course, but we wouldn't expect readers who find the articles irrelevant to act in response to the messages in the newsletter. And that's the rub. We publish newsletters for a reason, and without some likelihood that reading leads to the right kind of results, the newsletter fails.

When considering relevance, remember the distinction between features and benefits – between the inherent value of a product or service, and the consequences of adopting or using it. For example, membership in an association may have no value in itself, but benefits such as the opportunity to meet others, to learn new skills, or to stay current on some issue do have value. When a benefit occurs, the person for whom it occurred moves closer to his or her goal.

By emphasizing benefits, rather than attributes or features, we increase the odds that a reader will find relevance. For example, he might make a connection between using a computer and achieving his goals on his own. But if headlines refer to benefits – "Save Time!" – rather than features – "A Faster Processor" – the link is explicit and more likely to be perceived.

Credibility

So you have the attention of the reader. You have succeeded in convincing him, for the moment at least, that your relevant content might satisfy his needs in some way. The article presents a solution or direction that is of immediate interest to him. But will he trust your information, analysis, or recommendations?

We'll look at credibility from two perspectives. First, do readers think you know what you're talking about? Do you have facts, statistics, or other documentation for what you're saying? Do they think you have the experience or expertise to address the subjects you've selected? That's the first credibility issue, and it must be considered.

The second perspective involves the needs of readers. Will they think you understand their needs, or that you even recognize that they have needs? Far too many newsletters focus on presenting the publisher's points, without recognizing that the reader also has needs. Publications that fail to focus on reader needs become glorified brochures, rather than effective newsletters.

Involvement/interactivity

Traditionally, mass media communication goes in only one direction – from publisher to reader (or viewer, or listener). That makes the reader a passive participant in the communication experience: one who receives but does not transmit. And a passive participant, all other things being equal, is less likely to be influenced than an active participant.

An interactive experience, on the other hand, employs two-way communication, and generates more involvement in the message (again, all other things being equal). Examples of interactivity include crossword puzzles, the questions in a survey, and letters to the editor. In most cases, we assume that interest in the publisher's message increases with the level of interactivity.

Emotion

Suppose you publish a newsletter for a software company, and I'm on your mailing list because I bought one of your programs. If I recently spent an hour on the phone trying to reach your technical help staff, my emotions about your company won't be very positive. So, would you expect me to be more willing or less willing to read your newsletter?

Anger is just one of many emotions that affect willingness to read a newsletter. Emotions can be positive or negative, and even negative emotions may serve a purpose. We can, and often do, manipulate the attitudes and behavior of those around us by inflaming their emotions.

Emotional factors may develop independently of organizations, but still have an effect. During an economic recession, for example, widespread cynicism exists about the statements of business and political leaders. Generally speaking, though, these are short-term concerns and shouldn't have a lingering effect – positive or negative – on willingness to read a newsletter.

Consistency

Many of us would argue that we appreciate and value variety, that diversity stimulates us, or that we like the challenge of new ideas. Yet one of the most powerful determinants of human behavior is the need for consistency. This reflects the need to make all our mental positions, including ideas, values, and beliefs, consistent with each other. For example, a smoker might experience conflicts if she enjoys the taste and physical experience of smoking cigarettes, but also knows that smoking increases her chances of dying at an early age. This inconsistency will trouble her until she resolves it in some way.

For the reader, new information that conflicts with existing ideas may lead to loss of willingness. On the other hand, it also might provoke a positive or negative response that prompts her to read. If we know our readers well, we probably know how far we can or should go with new notions.

Multiple Dimensions

Over the course of the last few pages we have explored several different factors that influence a reader's willingness to read a newsletter. Of course, there are others we haven't considered, and some that are no doubt unique to your situation.

Perhaps we could identify and measure all of them, but that seems a rather daunting task when we consider the length of the list, and then the variables included with each of them. What we want, instead, is a broader sense of a reader's willingness to read our newsletter.

Indeed, we'll go so far as to make some generalizations, based on the type of newsletter. If you publish a marketing newsletter, then assume your readers are generally unwilling: even if they like you and your products, they are responding to the uncertainty inherent in making purchases. Membership newsletters, on the other hand, often can assume a willing readership. Member affiliation involves voluntary relationships among peers who share contributions and interests. And for employee newsletters, start by presuming that your readers are unwilling. While employees may share your vision of the organization's future, they may not share your ideas about how to get there, or how to share the rewards.

Able Readers?

It's one thing to have willing readers, but what if they're unable to read the newsletter? A reader who cannot understand either the individual words or messages – explicit or implicit – isn't likely to help us achieve our objectives.

So, once again we'll revisit our newsletter loop, and add another decision point, as shown in Figure 4–3. Is the reader able to read the newsletter? If yes, then we proceed as planned; if not, then we need to figure out why, and make changes.

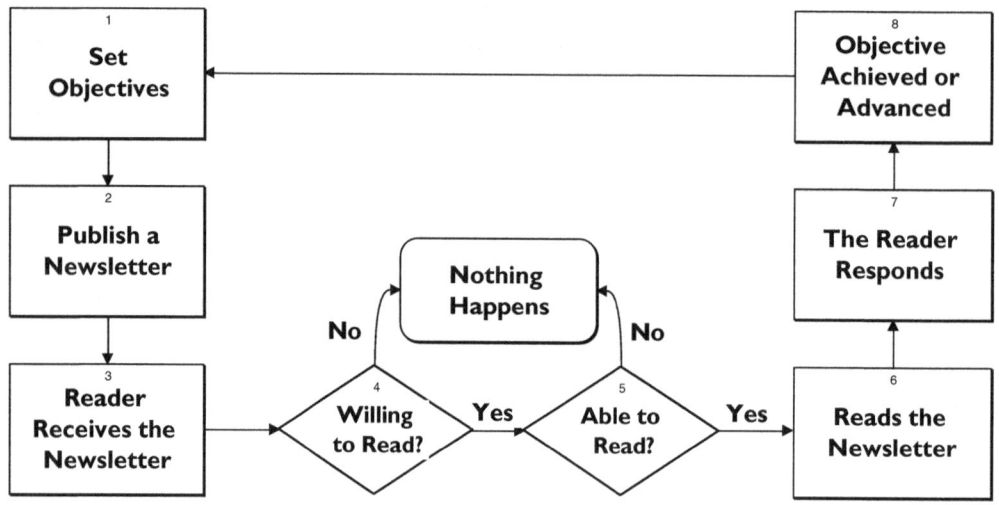

Figure 4–3

We'll examine four dimensions that affect reading ability:
- Reading competence and readability
- Availability of context
- Level of abstraction in the wording and symbols
- Structure of text, graphics, and design

Reading competence and readability

By reading competence, we mean the ability to understand individual words, and to understand the messages that the words convey in phrases and sentences. We often rate this ability by identifying the highest grade completed in school, college, or university.

While we have no control over reading competence, we can control readability – the extent to which the material is easy to read. Readability, of course, is the flip side of reading competence, and it is a variable we can adjust to match the capabilities of the reader.

In recent years, we've had a helpful aid for checking the readability of our writing. Grammar-checking software does it for us, and can make the task almost effortless. This software analyzes such measures as sentences per paragraph, words per sentence, and letters per word. In addition, many grammar checkers also count passive verbs. Whatever the measures, they give us a reasonable assessment of how easy our text is to read. This paragraph, for instance, has been rated by a grammar-checker as easy to understand for a person who has completed nine and a half years of schooling.

We acknowledge the controversy about the ability of grammar-checkers to correctly identify violations of grammatical rules. However, that shouldn't stop us from using the readability measures, as at least a rough guide.

Context

When talking about context, we're talking about the situation within which we place our messages. It involves circumstances, facts, and other information that help the reader understand the meaning of the message. Sometimes, we think of it as the framework within which an idea is presented. Without the context, we might not understand why something was written.

Readers also participate in context by bringing their own framework to certain ideas. "We see what we expect to see" expresses the way context affects us. Over time, we come to expect certain types of messages in certain types of situations.

Level of Abstraction

Ability to understand, for all but the most educated readers, will be lower for abstract words, and higher for concrete words. Abstract and concrete represent two ends of a spectrum, with intellectual concepts at one end (abstractness) and sensory experience at the other (concreteness). Words from the concrete end of the spectrum seem more familiar and allow fewer interpretations of meaning, making them easier to understand for most readers.

A related issue involves explicit versus implicit messages. Some words provide clear, direct images and meanings; others ask or allow us to fill in the gaps ourselves. Good fiction, to take an implicit case, offers words and images that can be interpreted in many ways, and as a result provides a rich reading experience. A product manual, on the other hand, uses explicit language and the careful manual writer aims to avoid ambiguity if possible. Many newsletter readers find explicit messages more readable.

Consider, as well, the explicit request — versus the implied request. As noted, newsletters exist to serve a purpose, one that may or may not be explicitly stated. Do readers understand what you want them to think or do?

Structure

Text structure refers to the way the message is put together. Rhetoric, the study of the art of influencing those who read or hear your message, deals at length with this issue. Should the most important argument come at the beginning or at the end? Will my position be stronger if I elaborate both sides of an argument, or if I simply ignore the other side? What's best? Again, it depends on audience and situation. If the concept of rhetoric intrigues you, look for books about it in your library.

Design structure deals with issues affecting visual perception. Good design increases readability by helping the reader. One way it can do this is by giving the reader's eyes frequent rests, with adequate white space (space not used for text or graphics). Like parks in a busy city, white space on a page allows us to rest or re-energize ourselves.

You will have noticed, too, that the size and style of type affects your ability to read and comprehend. Similarly,

- bulleted points highlight certain key issues, so readers grasp them quickly.

For example...

Employee newsletter: *Inside News*

Inside News, published for the employees of Transcontinental Printing, aims to help readers cope with rapid and far-reaching changes in the industry, the company, and their individual jobs.

Willingness
Readers themselves define relevance, in the annual survey of their preferences. While subject rankings change from year to year, three general categories consistently appear:
- Corporate direction and plans
- Changes that affect jobs and futures (such as new or changing technologies)
- Human interest stories or photos about fellow employees

Credibility comes from the sources of content in the newsletter. Articles about corporate direction and plans come from senior managers or quote senior managers. To keep readers informed about changes in technology and management practices, the newsletter either summarizes articles from respected industry publications, or interviews members of staff from appropriate departments. For example, employees or managers in sales might explain new or changing concepts such as team-based selling and strategic alliances. For human interest stories, credibility is not significant.

Neither are emotion, interactivity, and consistency significant for willingness. Humor is welcomed, particularly in the local plant news, which often focuses on human interest issues.

Ability
Ability does matter. The text of each issue gets checked to ensure it is at or below the Grade 10 level, so it is easy for readers to understand. In design, we try to keep each article visually distinct from other articles; few of them start on one page and continue on another, for example. Some articles go in text boxes, and others are set off from adjacent articles by type size. In addition, most articles are quite short, and we normally use only one level of subheading.

Membership newsletter: *Calgary Quality Council Faxletter*
The *Faxletter*, published by the Calgary Quality Council, was a tool for communication among peers, and so we would expect willingness and ability to be relatively high.

Willingness
As long as the newsletter dealt with issues related to Total Quality Management (TQM) or Quality Assurance (QA), the content was relevant to the readers. A desire to know more about those subjects, after all, led them to

join or consider joining the association. Still, we note that readers have different levels of familiarity, knowledge, and understanding.

Given the peer relationship, the newsletter had credibility when the content dealt with TQM or QA issues. This reflected the shared experience of members and potential members.

Turning to the three other dimensions of willingness (involvement, emotion, and consistency), we would expect mixed responses. Newsletters such as the *Faxletter*, which dealt with professional issues, tend to be informational, rather than seeking commitment or action on the part of members. So none of these three dimensions concern the publishers of such newsletters. On the other hand, publishers of a newsletter for a political party or an advocacy group might place more emphasis on these dimensions than on relevance and credibility. Involvement, emotion, and consistency are more likely to win the kind of commitment and passion required for causes.

Ability

We assume that readers shared the same general level of reading competence as those who published the newsletter, since the Council was an association of peers. While there were certainly variations in reading competence, they would have been relatively minor.

This newsletter, like most newsletters dealing with professional issues, aimed for an intermediate level of abstraction. Highly abstract treatments belong in academic journals or research papers, while at the other end of the spectrum, highly concrete descriptions are appropriate for how-to publications and manuals.

Structurally, a newsletter like the *Faxletter* aims for quick and easy consumption. Readers should be able to quickly identify and read the sections that interest them, and be able to skip over those that do not.

Marketing newsletter: *The Sovereign Report*

The Sovereign Report goes to insurance brokers across Canada. It helps The Sovereign General Insurance Company build and maintain relationships with brokers by providing information about marketing and managing.

Willingness

As we pointed out earlier, brokers face the challenges of competing with insurers who work through other channels (such as telemarketing and direct mail) and managing effectively in an industry with highly cyclical revenue and earnings. Generally, then, content focused on these two issues will be relevant.

It won't be the only source of information, or even the most important. Nevertheless, surveys indicate it is highly regarded by readers in the target audience.

Credibility is established by basing much of the content on features in other publications, mainly magazines and journals that enjoy respect in the insurance or wider business community. Some of *The Sovereign Report* articles summarize the original features; others build on an original feature, perhaps about another industry.

Senior managers of the company are the other major source of content. They have the credibility that comes with building a successful and growing business, particularly one in a highly competitive industry. That position is sustained by the trust a senior manager in a financial institution must possess.

Ability

We'll start by noting that a peer relationship exists between the managers of an insurance company and the managers of brokerages. They share, for example, similar levels of education and industry-specific training. In addition, career paths sometimes take them back and forth between brokerages and insurance companies.

With an emphasis on practical information about marketing and managing, the newsletter takes a middle course between abstractness and concreteness. If the information is too abstract, it can't be applied readily. If, on the other hand, it's too concrete, then readers won't know where it fits within the broader range of techniques and theories.

Finally, readers of *The Sovereign Report* are busy people. For that reason, the newsletter emphasizes short, easily understood articles. The front page displays one article, with about 300 to 350 words. The second page article also features one subject, a bit longer, but often using many bulleted points. Page 3 normally contains three or four short pieces, each set off from the others by white space and headlines.

Chapter 5
Selecting content

In this chapter...

When we select content for our newsletter, we want subject matter that does two things at the same time: It influences the ways readers think or act, and, it provides information that readers find helpful or interesting. We call this common ground the shared environment. Some subjects automatically emerge from the shared environment:

- Employees (readers) and their employers (publishers) share an organization and industry
- Product users (readers) and suppliers (publishers) share a product or service
- Members (readers) and associations (publishers) share an issue or a common cause

Subjects from the shared environment will be relevant to both reader and publisher, because both have something to gain from addressing them. And the reader knows enough about these subjects to judge the credibility of the material or the sources.

If we stay within the shared environment, both reader and publisher will be helped toward their objectives. And while the range of subjects we can cover may seem restricted, this is not true. If the boundaries of the shared environment do seem too narrow, the problem lies in the objectives you've set for the newsletter, and not with the scope of available content.

Further, we can take a micro approach to content, a macro approach, or both. These represent methodical ways of expanding the number of subjects within the shared environment.

A strategic approach to content

If you've been involved with a newsletter, you've probably heard the question, "What should we write about?" many times. You've probably asked it yourself a time or two. And it's a good question. Finding the right content can take more time and effort than any other single aspect of newsletter planning. It's also the single most important editorial factor in publishing a successful newsletter.

To some extent, we've already started defining the nature of appropriate content for newsletters through our discussions in earlier chapters. And in Chapter 12 we'll look at some very specific sources and methods. In this chapter, though, we deal with a critical issue – a framework for our ideas about content, and a set of criteria for selecting subjects.

We deal with this framework strategically. That is, we want subjects that help us (the publishers) achieve our objectives, by influencing reader actions or attitudes. And, keeping in mind our discussion in Chapter 3, we'll also make a point of serving readers with content they want or need.

Is it possible to do both – to satisfy both readers and publisher – at the same time? Yes! Indeed, that's the essential challenge of non-subscription newsletters. It's easy enough to publish brochures, which deal with just the publisher's needs, or subscription newsletters, which deal with just reader needs. Finding common ground – to serve both reader and publisher at the same time – may present a unique set of challenges or demands, but it also offers opportunities for effective communication.

A shared environment

This common ground that we've called the shared environment can be visualized with a simple Venn diagram, as in Figure 5–1.

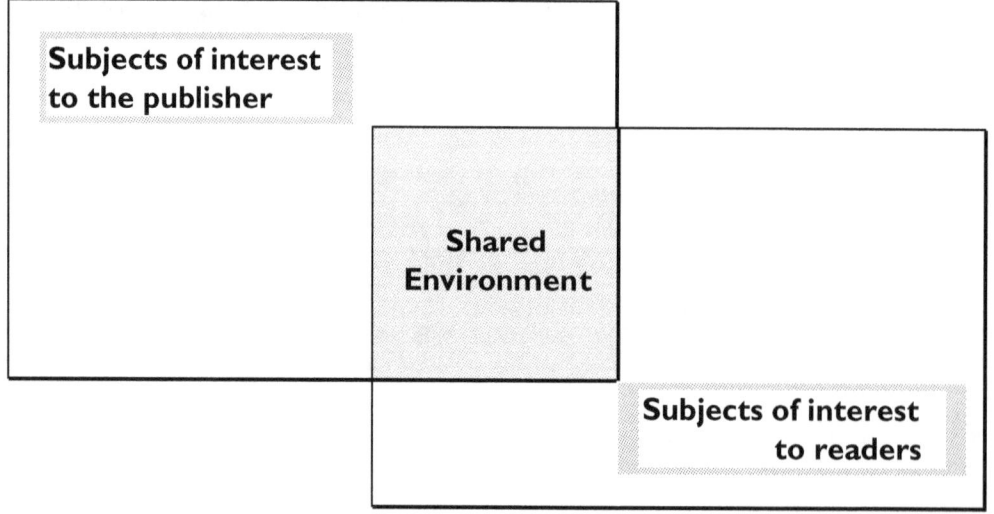

Figure 5–1

You probably recognize that subjects in one environment relate to the needs of the publisher, and that subjects in the other relate to needs of the reader. The first set of subjects helps the publisher get the reader to respond in a particular way; the second set helps the reader move toward her goals. What's new in this chapter is the overlap between the two – the shared environment.

Let's consider some examples. In the case of an employee newsletter, the shared environment would certainly include the organization. The publisher is usually management, which has an obvious stake in the organization's health and prosperity. But employees have an important stake, too. The organization provides them with a wage or salary and perhaps even a sense of purpose in their lives. Of course, employees and management may disagree about issues pertaining to the organization. But they still have a very strong shared interest in it.

For a marketing newsletter, the product that one uses and the other sells can be found in the shared environment. If you're the publisher, you probably publish the newsletter because you want more people to buy your product or service. If you are the user (or buyer), your productivity may depend on getting the most out of the product. The product makes up a critical part of your shared environment.

For a membership newsletter, the shared environment will include the interest or cause that prompted you to become a member, or to publish the newsletter. Associations formed to fight diseases, for example, publish newsletters because they want to help fellow sufferers cope with the disease, and they want a cure. Individual members want that help, and in turn want to help others.

These three examples point to issues at the center of the shared environment. But they're not alone in it. For members and membership organizations, secondary but important issues include fund raising and alliances with other organizations. For employees and managers, the shared environment also includes industry issues and national trends in the consumption of the product or service they sell. Every shared environment includes many issues – some obvious, some not so obvious. As a publisher, it's your job to identify them.

Note, though, that while publisher and reader share an environment, they experience it differently. If it's an employee newsletter, for example, we expect management (for whom the publisher speaks) to have one view and employees (readers) to have another. Think of salaries and wages, in which both parties share an interest. The parties often, and quite naturally, have different views about what amounts are appropriate.

Relevance and credibility

In discussing the shared environment, you may see a connection to relevance and credibility, as we presented them in Chapter 4. A subject relevant to both readers and the publisher falls within the shared environment, and would be considered a good subject for the newsletter. In other words, both reader and publisher have something to gain by exploring this subject (and perhaps something to lose by not addressing it).

And, if the subject comes from the shared environment, we expect both reader and publisher to have some knowledge of it. The publisher may have more in-depth knowledge of it than most of the readers, but the readers have at least enough knowledge to determine whether the information is credible, or comes from a credible source.

You may find relevance and credibility helpful in determining whether subjects fit within the shared environment. The idea of a shared environment, obviously, is somewhat abstract. Relevance and credibility, on the other hand, are more concrete and more easily established when assessing content ideas. You can filter content proposals with these two questions:

- Is this subject relevant to both publisher and reader?
- Are we a credible source, in the eyes of readers, when we discuss this subject?

Setting the boundaries

In each of the three types of newsletters examined we've seen a shared environment. For employee newsletters, it centers on the organization they share. Readers and publishers of marketing newsletters share a product or service. And, for membership newsletters, there are core interests or causes, and organizational structures shared by officers and members.

To define the boundaries of any shared environment, then, we need to identify what it is the publisher shares with the reader, and what she does not share with them. In effect, this exercise integrates the main issues we've discussed in the first four chapters.

In Chapter 1, we discussed supply and demand factors that led to the growth of newsletters as a prominent medium. Three demand factors – expectations among stakeholders, explaining complex issues, and niche audiences – also help us relate the boundaries to specific issues and audiences. What are the expectations, what are the issues, and who is included within that niche audience?

Chapter 2 introduced our objectives in terms of reader responses. Now we're ready to determine the area or areas within which we want to influence or persuade. Employers should want to influence the attitudes or actions of employees only about issues that involve their work. Sellers should want to influence the behavior of buyers only in areas where they have something to sell.

Reader needs were emphasized in Chapter 3, as we discussed the ways in which people use media in general, and newsletters in particular, to help them achieve their goals. A member of an advocacy association, for example, would expect to use a newsletter from this organization to address issues related to the shared cause. So, reader needs and interests are another element in setting the boundaries.

In Chapter 4, we looked at reader willingness and ability. As we saw, a publisher can use two key elements of willingness – relevance and credibility – to help establish boundaries. The same is true of ability – when we stay within the boundaries of the shared environment, the reader is much more likely to understand the language and context without assistance. And that's another clue for publishers.

Setting the boundaries of the shared environment, then, should not require guesswork. Instead, it should flow, almost automatically, out of decisions discussed in the previous chapters of this book. And, by staying within the shared environment, the publisher remains focused on what she wants readers to do, and on what she has a mandate to ask of them.

What doesn't fit?

Recipes, a staple of many newsletters, come to mind as an example of poor choice. Unless the publishing organization is in the food business, recipes are irrelevant, and in addition, the publisher has no perceived expertise in this area, and hence no credibility. Similarly, when publishers of marketing newsletters talk about their organizations, not their products, readers are not likely to find the content relevant.

You can add bowling scores to that list. The achievements of the company bowling team may interest a few other employees, but the tournament scoresheet is not likely to interest management, and it's certainly not likely to help other employees fulfill their needs or achieve their goals.

Personal announcements such as notices of births and marriages, may fit, however, in an employee newsletter. These may be relevant to other employees because, for instance, the news may help explain absences or the changed behavior of co-workers.

A good general rule is to avoid subjects whose presence in the newsletter needs explaining. If we need to explain why a subject is being included, we're probably straying outside the shared environment.

This general rule must be broken or stretched at times, but if you do break it, you should be able to articulate the reasons for doing so. And sometimes the correct approach, when we want to include a seemingly irrelevant subject, is to make it relevant by providing appropriate context.

Narrow straits?

Once we've defined the boundaries of our shared environment, we may begin to feel that we've drawn them in too tightly, and that there's too narrow a range of subjects from which to choose. But that isn't true. Remember, the newsletter exists to serve the objectives of the publishing organization. To achieve those objectives, the newsletter must affect the attitudes or behaviors of readers, whether by reinforcing or changing them. And those attitudes and behaviors will be part of that same shared environment.

A marketing newsletter can reasonably expect to influence behavior involving its product, but not behavior involving something from a different realm of the reader's life. An employee newsletter can legitimately aim to influence behavior on the job, but not behavior on the employees' own time.

Remember, too, that while our shared environment may seem tightly constrained, we shouldn't run out of subjects in an issue or two. The publisher can take a micro approach and look at narrowly-defined subjects in detail, or she can take a macro approach and work through broadly-defined issues and external influences that include or affect the subject.

Micro/macro

The micro approach to content means looking inward. For a marketing newsletter that might mean dealing with one product feature in great detail. An article might explain how the feature benefits the user, how it can be used, and how it differs from a similar or previous feature. For a membership newsletter, it could be an article explaining why the executive committee has decided to change the annual dues.

A macro approach, on the other hand, means looking outward. For an employee newsletter, it may mean an article on technological changes that affect all companies in the industry. For a membership newsletter, news about a lobbying alliance with another organization that shares the same principles, but not the same causes, would be an example. For a marketing newsletter, it may be a report on how a product is changing in response to new environmental regulations.

If, after considering both the micro and macro approaches, the range of subjects still seems too limited, then we need to think about enlarging the focus of the newsletter. That, of course, means revisiting the objective or strategy.

Another voice

A study on employee newsletters conducted for *Industry Week* magazine ("The Real Scoop," June 17, 1991) found what it called "a strong mismatch of CEO wants, employee interests, and actual content." Turning to what employees did want, *Industry Week* said, "Employees […] want information that helps them understand their work environment and their relationship to it. They want to read about:

- The company's future.
- The competition.
- Reasons for important organizational actions and decisions.
- The organization's goals and direction.
- Opportunities for career advancement.
- Product development.
- Employee benefits.
- The organization's strength and stability.
- Product-quality and quality-improvement efforts.
- The organization's financial results."

You'll note that each of these issues fits within the shared environment for an employee newsletter. Other reader surveys with which I have been involved over the past several years have generated results similar to those in this *Industry Week* survey.

For example...

Membership newsletter: *Calgary Quality Council Faxletter*

The shared environment of an association or not-for-profit organization starts with the interest or cause that prompted members to join. For the Calgary Quality Council and its members the issue was Quality, in the form of Total Quality Management and Quality Assurance.

Consequently, as long as this newsletter provided information linked to either of these subjects, the content remained relevant. The incentive for membership, or for readers to ask to be put on the Council's newsletter distribution list, was the opportunity to learn more about these subjects. In some cases, that's an opportunity to learn directly, while in others it's a way to find other sources of information that can be tapped.

The *Faxletter* emphasized the latter approach: It provided information about sources. In taking this approach, it needed to ask whether the referrals it provided were significant in themselves, or there was something new about them that would keep them relevant. For the publisher (the association), these issues were relevant because the investigation and adoption of Quality represented its purpose.

The *Faxletter*'s credibility can be attributed to its place as a communication vehicle for the executive members of the association. Members of the executive were leading members of the 'Quality community.' And the readers had at least a basic understanding of Quality, which enabled them to judge credibility.

In the same vein, we note that this newsletter often pointed readers to other organizations and sources of information. In this case, the credibility of the newsletter, and of the Council, depended on the integrity and usefulness of the organizations to which it made referrals. Generally, readers would assume the sources to be credible, because they had been listed by the Council. However, that credibility would be lost if readers discovered that the sources were not useful or reliable.

Marketing newsletter: *The Sovereign Report*

For *The Sovereign Report*, the shared environment comprises two sets of subjects: the marketing of property or casualty insurance, and business management.

Relevant content includes subjects like these:
- How-to articles on marketing, whether generically or in insurance agency-specific terms
- Case studies on individual insurance agencies, explaining what they've done and how
- Interviews with successful salespersons, or reports on the philosophies and techniques of sales leaders
- Reports on emerging management strategies
- Challenges and opportunities deriving from new technologies or trends
- Explanations of how ideas can be applied

These topics can be divided into micro and macro categories. For example, a case study article profiling an individual agency would be considered micro, since it deals with a very specific aspect of agency management. On the other hand, reports on emerging management strategies would fit the criteria for macro, since they deal with external forces that might affect any business or insurance agency.

There are several reasons why articles in *The Sovereign Report* are considered credible by targeted readers:
- The company has an excellent reputation in the industry, and consequently the newsletter has credibility by association
- There is constant interaction between the agencies and the company, so agency people generally expect people at The Sovereign to understand and respect their needs
- The ideas come from established, reputable publications
- The newsletter has been published regularly and continuously over a number of years

An aside

Since its inception, *The Sovereign Report* has included a letter from a senior manager on Page 4. Traditionally, letters from the president or a senior officer have been one of the scourges of newsletters, primarily because they often deal with subjects relevant to the publisher only. In this newsletter, though, the letters deal with subjects that are also relevant to the readers, and the source has credibility. That means they stay within the shared environment, and consequently make good content.

Employee newsletter: *Inside News*

The company, Transcontinental Printing, is what management shares with employees, but the company, of course, does not exist independently. It's part of a larger industry, and it works with other industries that are customers (retailing) and suppliers (such as the paper and chemicals industries). It also has vested interests in the well-being and job satisfaction of its employees and in the rewarding of its shareholders. In other words, even if the shared environment is just one company, the company has extensive linkages beyond its own walls.

Consider these content ideas:
- Employee benefits that affect employees and the company directly
- New equipment that has consequences and implications for both the company (managers) and for employees
- Health and safety issues. The well-being of staff has direct consequences for both employees and employers

- Social events. Though these are often on the borderline between relevance and irrelevance, in the case of *Inside News*, they add variety and a human touch to generally technical subject matter

Those issues, by and large, fit within the walls of the plants, and can be considered micro subjects. But there are also macro subjects that fit within the shared environment:

- Industry trends, whether technological, managerial, or environmental, affect everyone within this shared environment, and they affect other industries as well.
- Changing management practices, such as strategic alliances, partnerships, and Total Quality Management. Such practices usually develop outside the industry, then find their way into it as companies find value in their application.
- Issues such as career development and job satisfaction also come in to the newsletter from outside, first as abstract ideas, then as leading industry practices, and finally as common practices adopted throughout the industry.

When the newsletter deals with issues like these, the content is assumed to be credible, since part of the job of management (and, by extension, the editorial staff) is to identify and research these issues. And the newsletter increases its credibility in these and other areas by interviewing employees or managers who are experts on company or industry issues.

Chapter 6
Presentation tactics

In this chapter...

"How should we present the subjects we've selected for the newsletter?" is the central question of this chapter. In answering it, we work with three sets of reader characteristics that affect willingness: involvement, emotion, and consistency. You will recall we used the two other elements of willingness — relevance and credibility — to select content.

We also introduce a number of different ways of presenting content, which we call voices. They include: *challenge, analyze, entertain, consult, envision, empathize, advise, teach, interpret,* and *solve*.

Your choice of voice should be determined by reader characteristics – the level of involvement, the positive or negative character of existing emotion, and the degree of consistency between the beliefs of the reader and the ideas proposed by the publisher.

Involvement
- Low involvement: challenge, entertain
- Moderate involvement: consult, envision, advise, solve
- High involvement: advise, teach, interpret, solve

Emotion
- Negative emotion: challenge, analyze, empathize
- Neutral emotion: entertain, envision, interpret, solve
- Positive emotion: consult, advise, solve

Consistency
- Low consistency: challenge, analyze, interpret, solve
- Moderate consistency: envision, solve
- High consistency: consult, advise, teach

Willingness and responses

In this chapter we continue to focus on reader willingness. As you'll recall, a reader's willingness to read the newsletter depends on a number of factors, including relevance, credibility, involvement (or interactivity), emotion, and consistency.

In the previous chapter we explained how relevance and credibility help us identify subjects for the newsletter. In this chapter we use the other elements of willingness – involvement, emotion, and consistency – to determine presentation tactics.

Again, we want to maximize impact. First, we want readers to read the newsletter – that's crucial. And if we have relevant and credible topics, we've made a good start. Now, we want to maximize how much is read, and how carefully it's read, and those measures depend on the three other factors of willingness.

We do that by matching the characteristics of willingness with the presentation style that will maintain or increase a reader's willingness to read the newsletter. For example, if readers are angry about the newsletter or the organization that publishes it, we might use empathy. Or if readers are highly involved with the organization and its newsletter, then we'll try to maintain that state by advising.

We refer to these modes of presentation as voices, and their purpose is to provide appropriate responses to the willingness characteristics. We want appropriate responses because they will increase the influence the newsletter exerts over the way targeted readers think and act.

We start by recognizing the existing characteristics that readers bring to the newsletter, and then choose the voice or voices that will be most effective for

- Developing new attitudes
- Reinforcing existing attitudes
- Reinforcing existing behaviors
- Developing new behaviors

The voices

Ten voices are used in this book. And while the list should be helpful, it's not complete or exhaustive, nor is it arranged in any particular order, or ranked.

- Challenge
- Analyze
- Entertain
- Consult
- Envision
- Empathize
- Advise or Inform
- Teach
- Interpret
- Solve

Challenge
Directly confront the reader's beliefs, facts, or logic – a dangerous course in some circumstances because the effort may backfire. But it may work if significant change is required, and if the newsletter has skilled writers and editors. It is not subtle; it is confrontational and questions the status quo. It deals explicitly with a problem area and explains your perspective, without apology.

Analyze
Give reasoned arguments in favor of your position or against the position held by the reader. Where challenge presumes a shock assault against the reader's beliefs or knowledge, analyze presumes a calm, let's work together approach, in which you try to persuade by the application of logic. Work through the differences that exist, and help the reader develop a new set of beliefs or knowledge.

Entertain
Make your point indirectly or create a more receptive atmosphere by amusing or diverting the reader. This can increase interest in either the subject or the newsletter as a whole. Entertainment tools include humor, puzzles, contests, and cartoons.

Consult
Exchange ideas with readers, ask their advice, solicit their ideas, or take other measures that lead to a two-way flow of information. Surveys, simple questions, provocative questions, and contests are among the effective consulting tactics.

Envision
Paint a picture of future benefits that come from adopting your position. Help readers see how they will move toward their goals by doing what you ask of them. A vision usually refers to something well into the future, and may minimize current differences.

Empathize
Acknowledge the reasonableness of the reader's current position or sympathize with his situation. To that, add an explanation of how your recommendations lead to a better outcome. Empathy provides a platform for jointly

investigating opportunities through which you both benefit. It also provides an atmosphere for analysis or envisioning.

Advise or Inform
Present information without editorial comment, supporting argument, or added context. Simply present the material, or the facts, on the assumption the reader knows the subject and understands the benefits. Two basic approaches to this are expanded information and condensed information. Chapter 12 deals with these approaches.

Teach
Provide information, but go beyond that by transferring functional knowledge or skill to the reader. Newsletters often include instruction, which gives readers information about how to do something. That might include step-by-step details, analogies to something with which readers are already familiar, or even practice in something they can do already, but not as well as they would like.

Interpret
Advise the reader, but explain the meanings of the words or messages as well. In addition to translating from one language to another, interpretation might include providing context, simplifying wording, or explaining relationships among elements that may not be clearly related in the reader's mind.

Solve
Solve problems for the reader. This is another form of advising, with emphasis on removing a barrier that stands in the way of the reader doing what you want, or of achieving his goals. Some tools to consider are shortcuts, elaboration on methods, and presentation of crucial knowledge.

A word of caution
We've noted that teaching is an appropriate tactic for newsletters. But, having said that, we hasten to add that you must respect the reader's desire to learn from you. All too often, we hear from publishers or would-be publishers who feel it is their job to educate readers (or customers, or members, or the world at large) about something they consider important.

But we can't educate anyone without his or her permission. Readers will learn from us if they wish to do so – if what we can teach them is relevant, and we as teachers are credible. Ultimately, though, the decision to learn or not to learn belongs solely to the reader.

Characteristics and voices

Mix and match

Determining which voices to use will be somewhat more complicated than picking one or more of those listed here. Start instead with sets of characteristics, which is to say, a collection of important reader characteristics.

For any given reader, the set of characteristics includes an involvement level, an emotional inclination, and a degree of consistency-of-belief with the publisher. And, for any given group of targeted readers, there will be ranges of involvement, emotion, and consistency, rather than specific levels. That means our assessment will involve several steps.

First, we profile our readers as a group or groups, to consider their collective level of involvement, their emotions, and the consistency of their beliefs with ours. In most cases, we'll find characteristics spread across the spectrum, so it will be necessary to try to establish a mid-point on the spectrum for each of the three elements.

Second, we list the voices recommended for each category, and look for common applications. In the examples at the end of this chapter, you'll see that advising or informing comes up quite often. That's because readers of these newsletters are at least moderately involved in the subjects covered, that they bring generally positive emotions to the reading, and that the ideas presented by the publishers are generally consistent with those already held by the readers.

Third, we need to remember that readers change, and they may change because of the messages they see in the newsletter. So choices should be revisited from time to time, to ensure that they're appropriate for the current audience. That's another good reason for regular surveys.

Involvement or interactivity

Involvement refers to the activeness or passiveness of the reader in response to the content of the newsletter. Is the reader passive – relatively uninvolved? Does she simply glance at each page or read each article without interacting with its content? Or does she get highly involved, using the content to find ways of advancing her interests?

High involvement generally indicates deep interest: we've touched on a subject the reader can connect with her dreams or objectives. Of course, if we're defending the status quo, we may wish to keep involvement low, so that the reader doesn't start considering other arguments.

Low involvement: Challenge or entertain
- Sometimes a challenge, in the form of a shock or surprise, will be more effective than a series of reasoned arguments – if we want a change.
- Entertaining with quizzes, contests, and puzzles can make the reader more receptive.

Moderate involvement: Consult, envision, advise, or solve
- By getting the reader to give us her opinion, engaging her in a form of consultation, we increase her involvement with both the newsletter and its messages.
- The same result might be expected when she envisions a different future – one that was not apparent before she began the exercise.
- Advising generally supports the status quo, since the information is being submitted without any attempt to influence the reader.
- Problem solving can increase involvement by removing barriers that prevent the reader from understanding or doing something.

High involvement: Advise, teach, interpret, or solve
- Advising merely informs; it doesn't argue for or against any position – at least not with much passion – and isn't likely to change existing involvement.
- Teaching can sustain high involvement, by building on existing sets of ideas and extending a current mind set.
- Interpreting involves explaining how something should be understood, and may involve the setting of a new context for understanding.
- Problem solving also can reinforce, by proactively eliminating events or arguments that might change the way readers think or act.

Emotion

In most cases, we want readers to have positive emotions as a result of reading the newsletter. There are a number of reasons for this desire, but one of the more important may be the long-term relationship that should develop between the publisher and reader. We want to build positive emotions over the long term, and counter negative emotions.

Negative emotion: Challenge, analyze, or empathize.
- If negative emotions are deeply held, challenge may be the most effective remedy. A short, sharp argument may cause the reader to assess or reassess some strongly held position.
- Analysis, in contrast, sets out to change a negative emotion into a positive one by helping the reader think through a particular belief.
- Empathy helps the reader understand that the publisher will be a partner in overcoming problems that produced the negative emotion.

Neutral emotion: Entertain, envision, interpret, or solve
- Use entertainment to make readers feel better about themselves, about you, or about the position you represent.
- If the present state of affairs isn't satisfactory, envisioning a brighter future may be the antidote, especially if the current state of affairs requires the clichéd short-term pain for long-term gain.
- Perhaps a lack of emotion reflects an improper understanding of the state of affairs. In that case, interpretation will provide another way of understanding facts or events.
- If the lack of strong emotion reflects a sense of fatalism, then problem solving may return a sense of control, and in turn, a more positive emotion to the reader.

Positive emotion: Consult, advise, or solve
- With positive emotions in place, you can consult with readers to find out what will keep them in that state of mind.
- Advising readers is the right approach when we're going to leave well enough alone: we're not going to do anything that might lessen those positive emotions.
- Again, we view problem solving as a proactive approach, a means of getting rid of the factors that lead to negative emotions. Solving and consulting are often used in conjunction with each other.

Consistency

Are we asking the reader to accept something new, something at odds with what she now believes or assumes? The larger the gap between existing beliefs and those that we're asking her to accept, the greater our challenge. Consider low consistency to mean little agreement between publisher and reader, and high consistency to mean extensive agreement.

Low consistency: Challenge, analyze, interpret, or solve
- Our list of voices is the same as that used in situations of low involvement and negative emotion. As in those earlier cases, challenges can be considered the shock troops of ideas. On the other hand, analyzing is a more reasoned approach than challenging. Interpreting puts our context or viewpoint in front of readers for consideration, and problem solving means eliminating barriers to higher consistency.

Moderate consistency: Envision or solve
- Use envisioning to open new prospects for readers – prospects that will resolve differences between reader and publisher beliefs. Solve the problems that prevent the reader from finding congruency.

High consistency: Consult, advise, or teach
- Consulting with readers allows us to determine how we'll stay in step with them, or how we will help them stay in step with us. Advising means we'll simply inform readers, and won't risk opening up any issues that may lead to inconsistencies. And teaching enables us to build on existing consistencies.

Design and graphics

So far in this chapter, we've emphasized presentation from a text perspective, which is consistent with what most managers know and work with when they contribute their managerial expertise to a newsletter.

But remember that visual aspects of a newsletter also count. The design, or look and feel, can have a great influence on the way the newsletter is perceived. Colors, design intensity, type faces, and other factors all help create a suitable personality.

For example...

Marketing newsletter: *The Sovereign Report*
Involvement

We generally expect readers to be at least moderately involved, and often highly involved, in the issues covered by *The Sovereign Report*. The nature of the insurance business and the industry forces them to be highly competitive, and that generates interest in tactics for competitive advantage.

Given moderate to high involvement, suitable voices include consulting, advising, interpreting, and problem solving. Page 4 of *The Sovereign Report*, which features a letter from The Sovereign's Peter Parkin, often takes a consultative tone, and sometimes reports on face-to-face consultations that have taken place earlier. The other three pages and the *Supplement* usually employ the advising voice.

Emotion
We expect the emotions of readers (brokers) about the publisher (The Sovereign General) to be positive, given the relationship that exists between them. Thus, we use consulting, advising, and problem solving. Again, we see the appropriateness of the consulting approach on Page 4, and of the advising approach on the other three pages.

Consistency
The beliefs and values of readers should be reasonably consistent with those of the publisher. Not only do they share customers or clients, but they go through the same training and education programs, belong to the same industry organizations, and interact socially.

The voices for high consistency are consulting, advising, and teaching. Our remarks in the previous paragraphs hold here, and we'll add a note about teaching: Observe that if there is a high degree of consistency, the odds of readers being willing to learn from the publisher increase.

Employee newsletter: *Inside News*
Involvement
Involvement is generally high among readers (employees of Transcontinental Printing) and we want to maintain this level. Some voices that *Inside News* uses for this are advising or informing, teaching, and interpreting. For example, articles often provide not just news about the organization, but also explanations about what developments in the industry mean to the reader.

Emotion
Emotions range mainly from neutral to positive, which means we have two tasks. One is to make neutral emotions more positive, and the other is to maintain existing positive emotions.

The main voice for maintaining positive emotions is advising or informing, and that is the one most commonly used in *Inside News*.

And to build from neutral to positive emotions, the newsletter often consults with readers. In addition, it uses interpretation to help readers understand the reasons for the changes, stresses, and pressures of the modern workplace.

Consistency

With moderate to high consistency between the values of the organization and those of its employees, the voices include envisioning and problem solving (for moderate consistency), and consulting, advising, and teaching (for high consistency).

For *Inside News*, advising is the most commonly used voice and the most appropriate, given the level of consistency. There is no need to change reader attitudes or behaviors radically; rather, the idea is to maintain existing consistency. That makes advising appropriate for passing on details about new practices and tools, such as technologies, and for corporate news. These voices are also applied to articles on employee benefits, such as health and pension plans.

Teaching and problem solving are used as well, especially when the subject is health and safety. Employees and the company generally agree on the importance of safety and the means to create and maintain a safe workplace. Teaching can be used, and will be an effective voice, because employees are willing to learn from *Inside News*.

Membership newsletter: *Calgary Quality Council Faxletter*

This newsletter went to a list of self-selected readers. Every person on the list was there because he or she asked to be, either directly or by joining the Calgary Quality Council. It is reasonable to assume that these readers came to the newsletter with an existing high level of involvement, positive emotions, and beliefs that were generally consistent with those of the organization.

Involvement

With a high level of involvement, the voices or tactics available to us include advising, teaching, interpreting, and solving. The intention of the *Faxletter* was not to teach, but to help readers find resources that would enable them to learn on their own, or to learn from others who could offer experience, theory, or both.

Interpreting applied to some extent, particularly in setting context for certain TQM or QA concepts. For example, this voice might be used to explain the criteria for corporate and public sector awards.

Advising was the most common voice, since much of the newsletter's role was to inform readers about opportunities for participation in events and activities.

Emotion

Emotion, whether negative or positive, is not often a factor in newsletters about professional issues, such as the *Faxletter*. Nevertheless, we note that tools for maintaining positive emotions include consultation, advising, teaching, and solving problems.

Consistency

Again, we'll note that readers were self-selecting, and were likely to agree with most of the values held by the Council and expressed in the newsletter. While minor differences might exist about means, these differences were insignificant in light of the common vision of ends they shared. The three voices for high consistency are consultation, advising, and teaching; consultation and advising are used extensively in the *Faxletter*.

Chapter 7
How often? How many pages?

In this chapter...

This final chapter in the Tactics section addresses two issues: frequency of publication and page count or number of words. It, too, uses the concepts of willingness and ability, but in a different sense than in earlier chapters.

In this chapter we deal with *willingness to think or act,* while earlier chapters dealt with *willingness to read* the newsletter. We also deal with the *ability to think or act,* rather than with *ability to read*.

This chapter, then, rounds out our discussion of persuasion and influence by addressing what readers think or do after being exposed to a newsletter. And as you'll recall from earlier chapters, the goal of a newsletter is to influence (change or reinforce) reader attitudes, behaviors, or both.

Frequency should be determined by willingness to respond. If readers are willing to act or think as we suggest, then we won't need to publish very often – perhaps quarterly would be frequently enough for a printed newsletter. On the other hand, if readers are unwilling, then we must increase the frequency – perhaps to monthly.

The page count of a newsletter should be determined by the ability to respond. If readers are easily able to act or think as we recommend, then we won't need many pages – perhaps two or four for a printed version. But if they will have difficulty doing what we ask, then we need more pages, rather than fewer.

Willing and able – again?

In previous chapters, we discussed what subjects to select and how the subjects should be treated – so readers are willing and able *to read* our newsletter. But willingness and ability to read are not our only objectives: Readers also must be willing and able *to think or act* as we wish.

In this chapter, we explain how willingness to respond (think or act) dictates frequency (how often we publish), and ability to respond dictates the page count (number of pages per issue). Once again, we turn to our newsletter loop, revised as shown in Figure 7–1, to illustrate these important questions graphically.

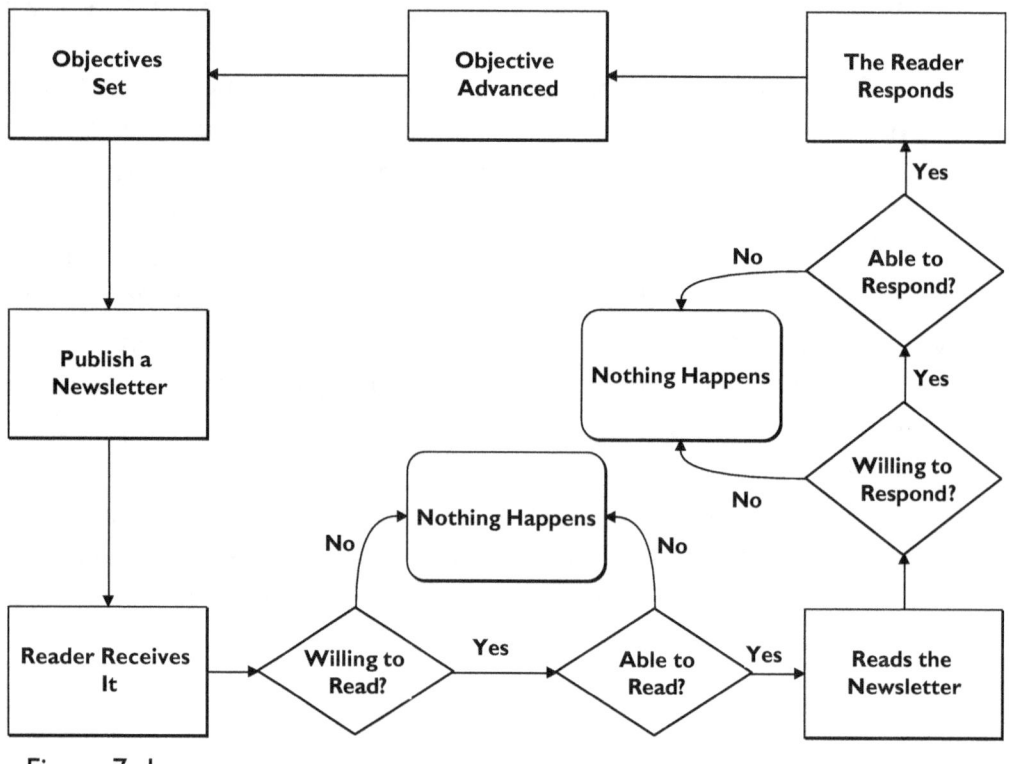

Figure 7–1

Let's start our analysis by reviewing some reasons why readers might be unwilling to respond to marketing, employee, and membership newsletters.

Marketing newsletters

In almost all buying situations an element of uncertainty affects willingness to respond. To one degree or another, buyers don't know what they're getting until they've committed their money, even with warranties, guarantees, or other protection.

An extension of this transaction-uncertainty principle is that readers can be expected to bring some degree of trepidation or skepticism to marketing newsletters. The degree is probably very high for expensive, infrequent purchases, and quite low for frequently purchased commodity-priced goods. The degree of skepticism or reluctance will generally reflect the amount of risk involved.

Employee newsletters

Employers and employees share a future, but their visions of that future and the way it will be pursued may be quite different. While their goals may be complementary, they can have distinctly different views about the means of achieving the ends, and about the sharing of rewards.

Thus, we expect readers to bring at least some degree of unwillingness to employee newsletters. The degree of unwillingness will vary from organization to organization, depending on factors such as history and culture.

Membership newsletters

For membership newsletters, unwillingness may stem either from lack of interest in the affairs of the organization or from reluctance to make a commitment. Many organizations, especially those that use a lot of volunteer labor, use newsletters to ask for help with tasks. But volunteering can require sacrifice, commitment, and the acceptance of unpleasant tasks.

Of course, unwillingness also may arise from other sources, including conflicting views about ends or means, styles of leaders vs. followers, and feelings of neglect or unwarranted attention. And if consistency levels for the organization (as expressed by its elected officers or staff) and a bloc of members is low, then some unwillingness will exist.

Frequency

Those are a few reasons why readers might be unwilling to respond to different types of newsletters. With that in mind, we can look at how this issue of willingness relates to frequency, or number of issues per calendar period.

The most common frequencies for printed newsletters are monthly and quarterly; and there is also bi-monthly (every two months), which is less common. These standards developed over time, and among many thousands of publishers, so we can say they're well tested.

Anything published less frequently than quarterly probably won't have much impact: It simply won't appear often enough to influence readers. At the high-frequency end of the range, few publishers expect gains from publishing more frequently than monthly. Conventional wisdom holds that readers will tire of a message if it's sent too often.

However, electronic publishing has made weekly, and even daily, publication common. For Internet newsletters, high frequencies may be better because competition for attention is much greater, and the odds of reader distraction are higher. Higher frequency also may be a function of the novelty of the medium, and the need to develop and spread knowledge about it.

Building a relationship

Having reviewed the common frequencies and some reasons for readers' unwillingness to respond, we now can explore the relationship between the two. As you would expect, the less willing the reader, the more often we need to make contact with her. To show how this works, we turn to the idea of exposures.

According to advertising theory, response to a particular ad depends on the number of exposures or impressions in a given time period. The assumption is that each commercial or display ad will get some response, but that the total number of responses will be greater than the sum of individual responses (in other words, greater than the number you would get by putting one ad into each of a number of different media). Each advertising exposure or impression has an additive effect, and the likelihood of an appropriate response increases with the number of exposures.

For newsletters, extra exposures do more than generate more impressions on the mind of the reader. Each issue can deal with a subject in a different way, giving us chances to try alternative approaches to it. An approach that misses one segment may connect with another. In short, more exposures mean more chances to influence readers.

But we also need to factor in time. The longer the interval between exposures, the more likely it is that the preceding message will be lost, forgotten, or superseded by someone else's message. An obvious example comes from marketing newsletters, which compete for the attention and response of potential buyers. Other suppliers may send newsletters, make sales calls, or advertise in the mass media, leading buyers to discount or overlook a message in our earlier newsletter.

Guidelines

In figuring out how often to publish, then, we see that higher frequency goes with greater unwillingness; lower frequency with more willingness. For example, if we assess our readers as quite unwilling, then we'd probably publish every month. On the other hand, if readers seem quite willing, then we might be able to publish quarterly and still meet our objectives.

Those seem reasonable conclusions for printed newsletters, but we can't speak of electronic newsletters with the same certainty. While the same principles should hold, we don't have a body of knowledge and experience about them in electronic terms. It may be that weekly takes the place of monthly and monthly replaces quarterly, but that is still a guess.

Considering all of these factors, we might hazard the following general guidelines:

	Electronic	Printed
Marketing newsletter	Weekly	Monthly
Employee newsletter	Monthly	Bi-monthly
Member newsletter	Monthly	Quarterly

Again, these are general guidelines; the frequency of your newsletter should be based on a careful assessment of reader responses, or potential responses.

From willing to able

If a reader is willing to respond to our newsletter, there is a good chance she will think or act the way we wish. But we can't take that response for granted. Instead, we need to consider the ability factor: Can the reader do what we're asking of her? Is she able to understand, and is she able to do? The answers to those questions determine how many pages go into a newsletter.

Let's consider some common types of ability and inability connected with different types of newsletters.

Employee newsletters

Often, employee newsletters aim to make employees more productive by getting them to do more, to act more efficiently, or simply to behave differently. But is what you're asking them to do difficult to accomplish? In other words, what capability do they bring to your objective, and how much more capable do they need to be?

A second aspect of employee ability also bears examination. Do readers (the employees) have the tools – training, better equipment, and so on – that will enable them to respond? Ability, then, is more than just the personal capabilities of the employee; it also involves the ability to access anything else that will make a response to the publisher's message possible.

Marketing newsletters

Marketing newsletters face several ability issues, including the ability of readers to access the product or service, to use it, to make the most of its functionality, and to pay for it.

For example, companies that sell costly products try to overcome readers' negative reactions to their prices by explaining the purchasing options available. They use their newsletters to present persuasive descriptions of their installment plans, lease contracts, and other alternative payment options.

Membership newsletters

If you belong to a non-profit association, you've no doubt heard debates about the ability of members to afford fees, or about how much to charge for events. If the association holds an annual conference in another city, directors need to ask whether readers are able to afford the transportation, accommodation, meals, and other travel expenses. If it appears that they might not be able to, the newsletter may be used to present cost-reducing ideas such as car pooling and to provide cost-reducing guides to low-cost dining and accommodation in the conference city.

And you can't overlook the perennial question asked by leaders of non-profits: "Why don't members participate more actively? Are they unable to take part, or don't they care?"

Ability and number of pages

Now we can build a link between ability and the number of pages. Again, intuition suggests that lesser degrees of ability require greater amounts of information – and the more information required, the more pages needed.

In the case of ability, though, we have access to more than intuition. We also can refer to our decisions about presentation voices, and base the number of pages on the voices we most frequently use.

Consider again the voices we discussed in the last chapter:

- Challenge
- Analyze
- Entertain
- Consult
- Envision
- Empathize
- Advise
- Teach
- Interpret
- Solve

If readers can do what's asked of them, we can use a voice such as advise, which won't require a lot of a introductory information (context), extensive justification, or complex explanation. If we use our newsletter to advise, a minimal amount of space is needed.

On the other hand, if we're asking readers to do something they can't easily do, then we need other voices. For example, to help employees or customers understand a new concept, we might analyze differences between the new one and the old one. That takes more space because we not only provide information (the advise voice), but we also explain how we arrived at our conclusions, and perhaps even present our methodology.

When multiple subjects exist, we're asking readers to do many different things, and the ability criterion applies to each one. From this, we can see that more subjects mean more pages.

Ability, and the reinforce/change distinction

One other tool might be useful in figuring out the page count: the distinction between reinforcing and changing. If the newsletter is expected to play a reinforcing role, a lesser number of pages will probably do the job. Changing, on the other hand, usually requires a greater number of pages.

If you have no other reference point in mind for a printed newsletter, start by visualizing a four-page version. If you want to reinforce, you can probably handle up to four subjects, assuming you'll be mainly advising. If your newsletter has tightly focused objectives, you might even drop to one or two pages.

On the other hand, if you want readers to change, you probably won't want to tackle more than a couple of subjects at a time in a four-page newsletter. You'll need extra space to argue your case, you may need to include graphics to illustrate the argument, and of course you'll need more repetition than for reinforcing.

Guidelines

Once more we'll venture some general guidelines, using them as reference point as we develop our own page counts based on the number of objectives set for our newsletter.

	Change	Reinforce
1 Objective	2 pages	1 page
2 Objectives	4 pages	2 pages
3 Objectives	6 pages	3 pages
4 Objectives	8 pages	4 pages

"But what about costs?"

Don't costs come into our calculations about frequency and number of pages? After all, more pages and higher frequency usually mean higher costs.

While we respect these cost factors, we also note they should have been built in – implicitly, at least – when the decision to publish was made. If the newsletter was created to achieve specific objectives, then the people who set the objectives probably had some sense of the costs and benefits involved.

If the objectives are significant, then the allocation of resources should reflect that. If the resources can't match the objectives, then the objectives can be prioritized, scaled back, or fulfilled over a longer period.

Of course, many newsletters don't have that kind of focus. They simply evolved or grew out of a manager's good intentions. If nothing else, then, working out a strategy for frequency and page count will force us to articulate and quantify our objectives. That may be working backward, but it's still worthwhile.

Essentially, then, we should let objectives drive the frequency and number of pages, rather than cost.

For example...

Employee newsletter: *Inside News*

Inside News, an eight-page newsletter, goes to employees of Transcontinental Printing an average of six times a year.

Frequency

Although the frequency varies, employees usually get about six issues. Objectives include helping employees understand new technologies and ways of working (including new methods of managing). And these methods and technologies involve a continuous flow, rather than one event or a series of events. New technologies, strategies, and methods enter the industry, undergo revisions, and are applied. Then there are more revisions, and the revised versions become the base for newer technologies.

Given this constant flow, even enthusiasts for new methods and technology need encouragement at times, while those less sure about the technology need regular support. So the willingness to respond – particularly the willingness to accept new technologies – requires relatively frequent communication. A frequency of six issues per year serves that need, although twelve issues a year might be more effective.

Page count

A web printing plant has a number of distinct departments or functions: Press operators run the presses, pre-press staff prepare the work that goes onto the presses, and finishing crews work with the printed material as it comes off the presses. Sales, customer service, administration, and other functions require additional personnel. Each function experiences a new technology differently, and sometimes only those in a single function or a few functions will feel the impact of the introduction of a particular technology.

As a result, many different messages about methods and technologies exist at any given time. *Inside News* generally allocates several pages of each issue to photos and stories about local events, and within this context, five pages of news about management and new technologies has generally been adequate. However, if the newsletter's mandate changes – from advising to encouraging faster adoption, for example – it will need to add pages.

Membership newsletter: *Calgary Quality Council Faxletter*
The Calgary Quality Council's *Faxletter* was a two-page newsletter, distributed by fax, normally ten times a year (monthly, except for July and August).

Frequency
One of the *Faxletter*'s main functions was promotion of the Council's monthly presentations or events. In addition, the Council considered itself a clearinghouse for information about other organizations' events, and many of those events were monthly as well.

Therefore, a monthly newsletter was most likely to get readers to respond. In each newsletter, readers could see what sorts of events were available in the coming month. A bi-monthly or quarterly newsletter might have been as effective as a membership tool (the other main function), to get existing members to renew or non-members to join, but not as a producer of willingness to attend events.

Page count
The *Faxletter* itself contained few articles designed to teach readers about Quality. Rather, the newsletter pointed readers to various other sources of information. As noted, the newsletter's main role was to inform readers about events and resources available to them. With the emphasis on advising readers, a minimal amount of space was required: two pages served adequately.

Marketing newsletter: *The Sovereign Report*
The Sovereign Report is a four-page newsletter, published six times each year (every two months). In addition to the four regular pages, the newsletter sometimes includes a two-page *Supplement*.

Frequency

The main objective has been to reinforce the good relations the company has with its select group of brokers, and reinforcement suggests less-frequent publishing. At the same time, we've noted a general unwillingness among readers of marketing newsletters, because of the inherent uncertainty involved in making purchases.

Given these two factors, the decision to publish bi-monthly seems sound. Had it been just a matter of reinforcing, quarterly publication probably would have sufficed. Or, had it been a case of changing the relationship (a task many marketing newsletters must assume), monthly might have been more appropriate.

Page Count

Making readers able to do what we want them to do is not a key factor for *The Sovereign Report*. Brokers already know a great deal about marketing and selling insurance products, and about managing their businesses. The newsletter does not provide basic knowledge about these disciplines; it provides incremental or supplemental information.

Often, the newsletter offers a glimpse of new marketing or management strategies, making brokers aware of them before they become common in the business community. In the case of the Parkin letter (on Page 4), it lets brokers know about the thinking of senior management at The Sovereign General. In other cases, the newsletter provides information from a wide range of periodicals – wider than most brokers would normally see – about the practices of managers in Canada and elsewhere.

Three pages provide enough space for the essence of a few new ideas, and for follow-up on these ideas for those who choose to pursue them. The fourth page, with the Parkin letter, deals with company thinking about issues in the relationship, and one page carries enough content to explain that thinking to the brokers.

Finally, the *Supplement* offers additional space for The Sovereign General to promote products or practices that reduce claims. Again, the amount of space is appropriate for presenting what brokers need to know, and making it possible for them to respond.

Section 3: Administration

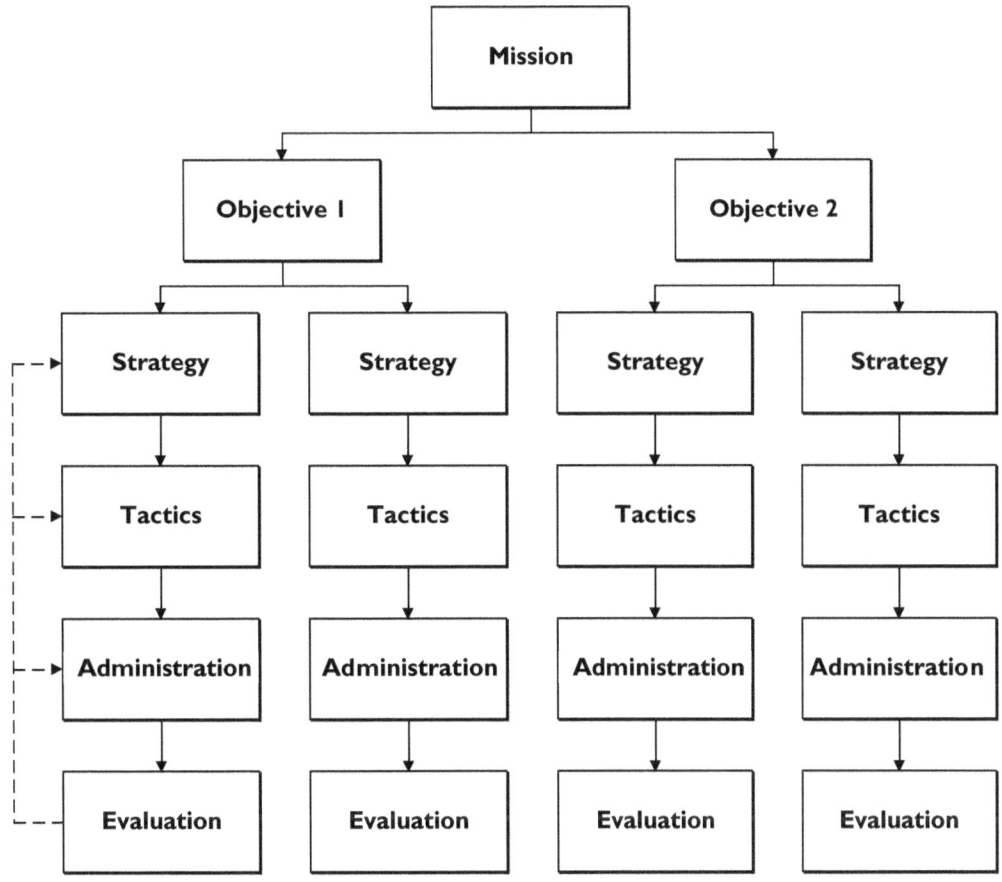

In the two previous sections, *Strategy* and *Tactics,* we dealt with planning issues, setting a foundation before publishing.

In this section, we work with a number of issues that will concern you as you leave planning behind and move into operations, or regular publishing. We deal with the following issues:
- *Management:* The structure and functions of an editorial board (Chapter 8)
- *Process:* A review of the full publishing process, from planning through evaluation (Chapter 9)
- *Budgets:* Developing a full set of budgets for a newsletter (Chapter 10),
- *Media relations:* Leveraging the value of your newsletter with other media (Chapter 11)
- *Story ideas:* Systems and sources for generating story ideas (Chapter 12)

At this point, our presentation changes slightly as well. While you'll continue to see a summary at the beginning of each chapter, you will not find the *For example* sections at the ends of them.

Chapter 8
Editorial Boards

In this chapter...

An editorial board is a group of persons who share an interest in the newsletter. Bridging the interests of senior management and the interests of the newsletter staff, board members make policy, supervise and evaluate, and support the editor:

- Policy aligns the work of the editor (and newsletter staff) with the operations of the department and of the organization as a whole. In other words, it links strategy and tactics with operations.
- Supervision and evaluation ensure compliance with these editorial and operational policies. Supervision refers to the ongoing process of control, while evaluation is a periodic exercise, in which we compare outcomes with objectives.
- Support for the editor means acting as a resource, and consequently extending the range and depth of editorial reach.

Your editorial board should include persons who represent stakeholders, and especially those who can speak for important reader groups. The composition of the board also should reflect the function of the newsletter. And representatives to the board should change from time to time: Establishing a systematic replacement policy is highly advisable.

Another important observation: While a board can and should help an editor, it should not usurp the role, authority, or responsibilities of the editor.

Why and what

If you or others in your organization have worked out the strategy and tactics of your newsletter, you've made real progress. But that doesn't mean you can hand over the job to an editor or writers. Before you can do that you need to set up systems to ensure that the newsletter gets started properly, and that it stays on track after it gets rolling. That's where an editorial board fits, as illustrated by Figure 8–1.

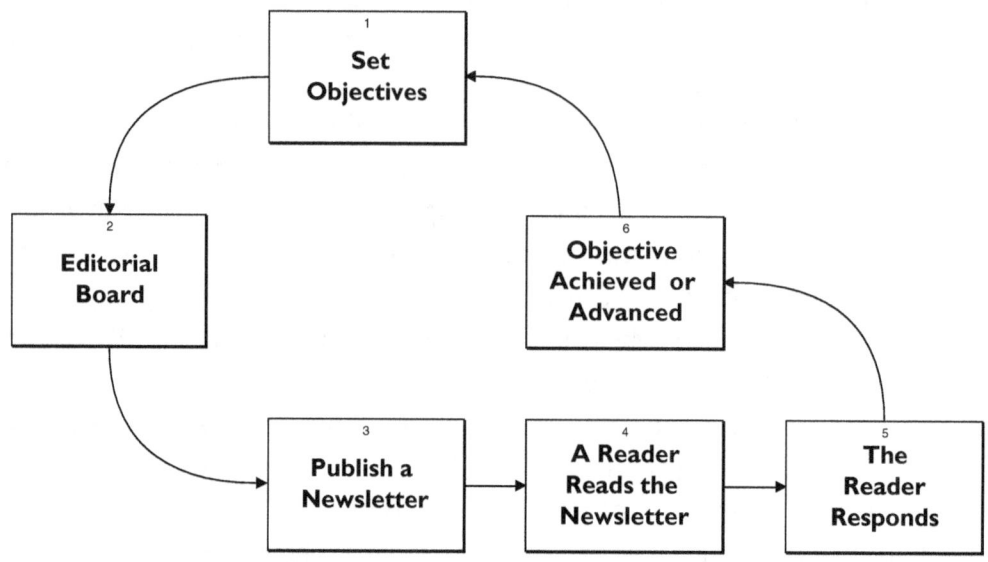

Figure 8–1

The board can be a formal group, precisely structured, with specified lines of communication and responsibility, or it might exist as an informal group of managers and employees who get together from time to time to solve pressing problems.

Whatever its structure, an editorial board is essentially a group that meets to establish and maintain the newsletter. It may have any number of roles and tasks, but most can be included within three general categories:

- Policy making – to align newsletter strategy with the organization's or department's goals
- Supervising and evaluating – to ensure compliance with the editorial and operational policies, and to assess the results
- Providing support – to make additional resources available to the editor.

Policy making

Terms of reference

By *terms of reference*, we mean the policies and procedures a board sets for its own activities. Policies are the rules and regulations that govern the activities of a board. The terms of reference might include answers to these questions:

- How often will the board meet?
- Will the meetings be formal, with an agenda, minutes, and rules of order?
- Who will chair the meetings?
- How involved will the board be in the operations and supervision of the newsletter?
- What kind of relationship will the board have with readers?

The answers to these and similar questions will define the policies of the board. You also might consider the policies of the organization as a whole, and how they fit with the policies of the board.

Procedures refers to the way the activities will be performed. For example, will someone take minutes of the meetings? Will they be distributed afterward? In general terms, policy refers to *what*, and procedure refers to *how*.

The setting of terms of reference probably doesn't need much attention in most organizations, since the board's management style will come to reflect the culture of the organization, regardless of the terms of reference.

Implementation

Whether you're planning a new publication or revitalizing an existing one, you'll want to meet objectives generated in the strategy stage. And moving from strategy to operations introduces many questions and issues that might not have been apparent to the strategists. Strategy provides a direction, but not specific policies and programs for day-to-day operations.

We can illustrate this with a hypothetical example from a distribution warehouse that is starting a newsletter for employees. In this example, we take an objective (one of a number of objectives) from the overall strategy, then develop policies and tactics that lead to fulfillment of that objective.

A. Objective (developed by a management team):
- Increase employee receptiveness to technological change.

B. Policies (developed by the editorial board):
- Allocate about two pages of each issue to technology, especially new machines and materials.

- Explain the links between new equipment and external forces of change.
- Whenever possible, include the comments of knowledgeable managers and employees.
- Measure knowledge of new technology, and attitudes toward it, in an annual survey.

C. Tasks (for the June issue, as planned by the editor)
- Do a story on the new packaging machine installed in April, explaining what it does and why it is better than the machine it replaced.
- Get a photo of an employee using the machine.
- Add an abstract of a magazine article that explains the importance of good packaging.
- Ask Supervisor Jane Smith to explain the importance of the increased capability. Interview salesperson Fred Brown about how it will increase customer satisfaction.

This hypothetical example shows how an objective becomes increasingly specific, eventually generating concrete operational instructions. Note that when the objective was formulated, there was no reference to how it would be achieved through the newsletter; in fact, it may not even have been exclusive to the newsletter. Perhaps the objective was developed as part of a general communication strategy for the organization, and affected all communication and educational systems.

Policies, on the other hand, do relate specifically to the newsletter; it would be difficult to imagine them being used in any other area. Unlike objectives, policies provide guidelines, priorities, and procedures the editor can use in her planning and assignments. However, they do not specify how the work will be done. Policy issues might include

- Guidelines on what subject matter will or will not be covered
- Allocation of space among various subjects, and the placement of subjects (such as the front page or center spread)
- Management approval – specifying what subjects need approval, and by whom, before publishing
- Equity – specifying, for instance, that a newsletter serving several locations of the same company will give an equal amount of editorial space to each location
- Criteria for the general appearance of the newsletter, if appearance is critical. For example, an architectural firm might want right margins

justified (even) rather than ragged, because of the implicit message that justification sends
- A fact checking mechanism, possibly linked to the management approval measure
- Success and failure criteria – if the board is to evaluate how well the newsletter has accomplished its mandate (an issue we explore later in this chapter, and in Chapters 9 and 15)

In developing policies, more perspectives usually provide better results. Generally, at least one member of the editorial board should come from the management team that set the objectives. He or she will be able to elaborate on implicit aspects of the strategy. Other members might represent affected readers or departments and be able to explain their interests and needs. Out of this mix should come a set of workable and effective policies, which the board turns into guidelines that help the editor make decisions.

Supervision

While policy making gets done infrequently – probably once a year at most – supervision goes on routinely and evaluation takes place at regular intervals. Supervision and evaluation, of course, are normal managerial functions.

Supervision

Within the framework of supervision, editorial boards can contribute to the success of their newsletters in three main areas:
- Budgeting
- Policy compliance
- Evaluation

Budgeting and spending

On the face of it, budgeting should be a relatively simple process, one in which we put in numbers for each line of identified cost. It's not simple in practice, though, because no cost can be assessed without also considering the assumptions behind it.

Preparing a budget often works best when done by a group, rather than an individual, and this is especially so if some members of the group have contact with senior officers of the organization and others have contact with targeted readers.

Broader exposure brings in more viewpoints, and that should generate not only cost-efficiency, but also greater acceptance by the manager who is accountable for the newsletter budget.

Compliance with policy

In terms of policy compliance, editorial direction might be the most important issue. Does the newsletter serve the needs of targeted readers, as well as those of the organization? Are appropriate tactics being used?

The same holds for supervision of general newsletter operations. Is staffing appropriate? Are we using reputable suppliers? Has the mailing list been updated to account for new customers or employees? Such questions are a matter of good governance and accountability, and require supervisory attention.

Evaluation

Management wants to feel confident that newsletter operations are well governed, to know that the organization receives good value for the money it invests in the newsletter. To whom can it look to for evaluations of the newsletter's contributions or impact? An editor, obviously, has a vested interest. Other managers may not have enough knowledge of the newsletter's purpose and operations, or may be subject to known or unknown biases.

While some of these shortcomings also might be found among editorial board members, as a group the board can be expected to function as forthrightly as any other committee or team. Further, reports about the newsletter's value should have credibility if they come from a group that includes both representatives of management and representatives of targeted readers.

And we can't overlook the question of time. Any useful evaluation requires time to solicit opinions and suggestions, to collect and tabulate data, to analyze the findings, and to write the report. An editor who operates on her own, without a board, will need more time than one who can call on board members for help with the project. And board meetings provide an opportunity to get opinions from various sets of stakeholders in one place, at one time.

Support

We make a distinction here between supervision and support by noting that supervision implies an arms-length relationship with newsletter staff. Support, on the other hand, suggests a peer relationship between the board and the staff.

The functions described in this section are those in which an editorial board works with the editor or staff to make the newsletter more effective.

Schedules

Getting a newsletter prepared, printed, and distributed on time is always a challenge, but an editorial board can help. First, the board can ensure a realistic and appropriate schedule, given the human and other resources available.

Second, members of a board can offer their expertise. If an issue is stuck because of a missing article, a member might write an article to substitute for the missing one. Newsletters face many obstacles between conception and delivery, and resourceful boards can help get issues out on time.

Third, if the newsletter regularly comes out late, the board can investigate and make recommendations or institute changes that will put publication back on schedule.

Spending

Often, an editor faces special situations that require a significant variation in the budget. Perhaps a senior manager wants a report from a conference, or a special edition introducing a new product. An issue of an employee newsletter might need four extra pages, in order to explain a new benefits plan.

From time to time newsletters need extra funds, and a senior person must be convinced the request is valid, or that the amount of additional funding is appropriate to the task. If a request for funds comes from the editorial board, we expect it to have more credibility than one that comes from the editor alone.

An editorial board also can bring one of the important strengths of teamwork into play: Putting more minds to work on a problem increases the number and quality of potential solutions. For example, if getting news from a distant conference without extra funding becomes a priority, perhaps a member of the board knows someone who will attend and could bring back notes and photos.

With a board in place, senior management has greater confidence that spending will be responsible, and with that confidence should come greater support for the newsletter. A team, and especially one with management representation, offers more accountability.

Resources

Another potential contribution comes from a board's range of contacts within the organization. Every editor or writer who sets out to develop a story needs the names of contacts and potential interviewees to get the assignment started or completed. The greater the diversity among members of the board, the broader the net for finding such contacts.

By having members placed strategically throughout the organization the board has access to many more potential sources than a single person. And in many cases, a writer finds it helpful to have an introduction to a potential interviewee, a task that can be handled by the board member who provides the reference. Further, as the range of expertise on the board expands, so does the likelihood that the content will reflect the range of issues that is important to readers.

Other contributions

Editorial boards can help the editor make the newsletter more factually accurate. When more people are involved, the odds increase that facts – and the inferences drawn from them – will be accurate. Fact checking is part of the editorial process in major magazines. While newsletters rarely have the resources of these magazines, they can ask board members to use their internal networks to check facts, make sure that the final version of the copy is accurate, and handle other corroboration tasks.

Another potential board contribution comes from the sense of connection board members can develop with people and departments that otherwise might feel excluded. The larger the organization or the greater the geographic dispersion, the more important this contribution becomes. Employees outside head office or customers beyond the main market area dislike perspectives that reflect only head office views.

Editors sometimes face pressure to allocate more space to special interests, voice more orthodox editorial opinions, or otherwise cater to critics. An editor who has the backing of a board enjoys a much stronger position in dealing with outside requests, suggestions, and criticisms. A board's decisions are more acceptable than those of a single individual: A formal board structure suggests consideration of all important views and a rational decision based on discussion or debate.

Creating an editorial board

An editorial board is what you make it. Whatever its structure or character, though, it should be capable of guiding the newsletter toward specific objectives and desired performance levels. Normally, this means appointing persons to the board who have something to offer, and who can articulate stakeholder views, especially those of readers.

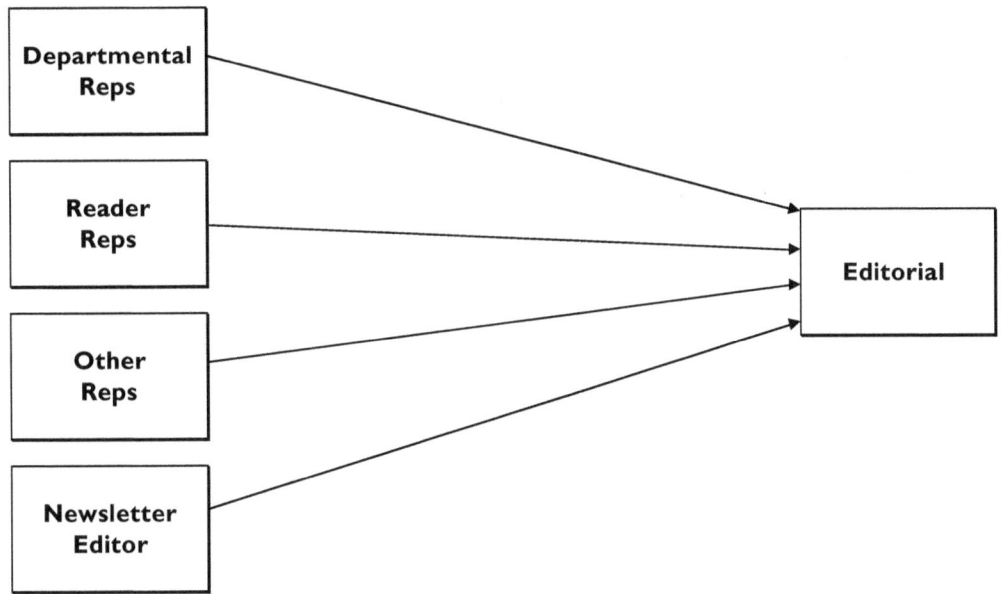

Figure 8–2

As Figure 8–2 shows, an editorial board should include representatives of key departments or functions, readers, and other stakeholders. The editor, of course, should be a member of the board and normally would chair the meetings. Other members of the board might include key contributors or outside advisors. The number of members depends on circumstances: too few means more work for each member or limited activities by the board, while too many means unwieldy meetings and confusion in assignments.

When looking for reader representatives, aim for key segments. Some examples of representatives for an employee newsletter might include

- Employees in different trades, departments, or functions
- Employees from different locations, whether within a region or within a big building
- Members of appropriate committees

In the case of a marketing newsletter, some examples of reader representation include

- Customers
- Sales representatives
- Front-line staff who deal regularly with customers

For a membership newsletter, I would suggest

- A representative of the Board of Directors
- An officer of the organization
- The Chair of the membership committee
- Representatives of major internal groups or perspectives

Throughout this chapter, we've stated that a board has an important role in ensuring that management's intentions and strategies are clearly and consistently expressed to the editor. Management representation on the board is critical, and might include
- The Sales Manager, for a marketing newsletter
- A Human Resources manager, for an employee newsletter
- An elected officer of an association
- Someone involved with public relations or corporate communication
- A representative of senior management

One other note about boards: If you have difficulty getting contributions from some locations in an organization with several or many locations, perhaps something like a sub-editorial board would help. A small group at each location can be responsible for finding and encouraging contributors. This sub-board would not have policy-making powers, but might instead act as an advisory council. It might contribute in many of the ways outlined in this chapter, without having to interpret strategy or create policy.

Recruiting

Recruiting a board can be done in either of two ways. You can prepare a list of persons who are considered good candidates for some set of reasons, and then try to persuade them to join. Or you can ask for volunteers, perhaps specifying some qualifications. Each approach has advantages and disadvantages, and the one you choose should reflect the culture of your organization.

Regardless of the approach, potential members will want to know what they gain from participating. After all, they will be expected to take on extra duties and responsibilities. However, potential members should enjoy many important benefits, including these:
- Being part of a team that produces something with a high profile within or beyond the organization.
- Gaining a better understanding of communication processes and communication management. Given the often-declared importance of communication, board membership offers good career credentials.
- Acquiring a broader perspective on the organization and its objectives.
- Having the opportunity to develop contacts throughout the organization, and perhaps beyond it.

Service on an editorial board provides skills, experience, and contacts that lead to job satisfaction and advancement. For most recruits, these benefits – and others unique to your organization – will more than outweigh the few hours of work per issue normally required.

Changing the board

A board that consistently fails to meet the goals set by senior management obviously must change. But even boards that work well should change from time to time.

Assuming the board works at least moderately well, consider regular and planned changes in membership. Such a policy prevents the board from becoming too settled, and ensures that new ideas and personalities come in regularly. The requirement that the board consist of a diverse and representative group of members makes changing it more difficult. However, changes also create opportunities to enhance positive aspects.

One approach involves some cyclical or rotational system. Perhaps a third of the members step down each year, after serving one term. That produces stability, while at the same time bringing in new members and new ideas.

These changes should not be too difficult if a system exists, and the board uses it to ensure an orderly and consistent transfer of membership among interested stakeholders.

A few words of caution

Although an editorial board has a mandate to make the newsletter effective, members should avoid getting too involved in day-to-day activities. The editor and newsletter staff should make decisions about the implementation of editorial policy, using their professional judgment and experience.

An editorial board that becomes too involved in day-to-day tasks does no good. Like other managers, the editor of the newsletter should be able to manage her function without undue interference or influence. If the newsletter is not meeting expectations, it is important to be sure the editor understands the criteria, and receives a specified time (and resources, if necessary) to make changes.

Chapter 9
Newsletter processes and scheduling

In this chapter...

The publication of a newsletter takes us through a relatively standard process, regardless of its type, length, or other characteristics, and includes:

- Annual planning
- Planning for each issue
- Editorial management
- Layout activities
- Proofreading
- Printing
- Distribution
- Payment of suppliers
- Evaluation

This chapter provides an overview of these processes. And, consistent with the discussion in the last chapter, it doesn't attempt to train you as an editor, although it looks at issues from an editor's perspective. Instead, the aim is to help you understand the tasks and functions involved in creating and publishing a newsletter.

These processes obviously don't fit every situation, but they do provide a generic model from which distinct models can be developed. And we try to be helpful by outlining them in checklist form.

As a manager or a member of an editorial board, you might expect to participate in the Planning and Evaluation sections, but otherwise, the activities here are generally the responsibility of the newsletter staff.

An overview of the process

If you're a member of an editorial board, you'll want at least a basic understanding of how a newsletter gets put together. But unless you've received some good hands-on help, you'll probably end up with bits of information, snippets which may or may not give you an accurate picture of what's involved.

In this chapter, you get an introduction to the newsletter publishing process. Your newsletter may go together differently, but generally speaking, most newsletters will go through a process somewhat like the one shown in Figure 9–1 below. Having this introduction should help you to budget for, supervise, and evaluate the newsletter.

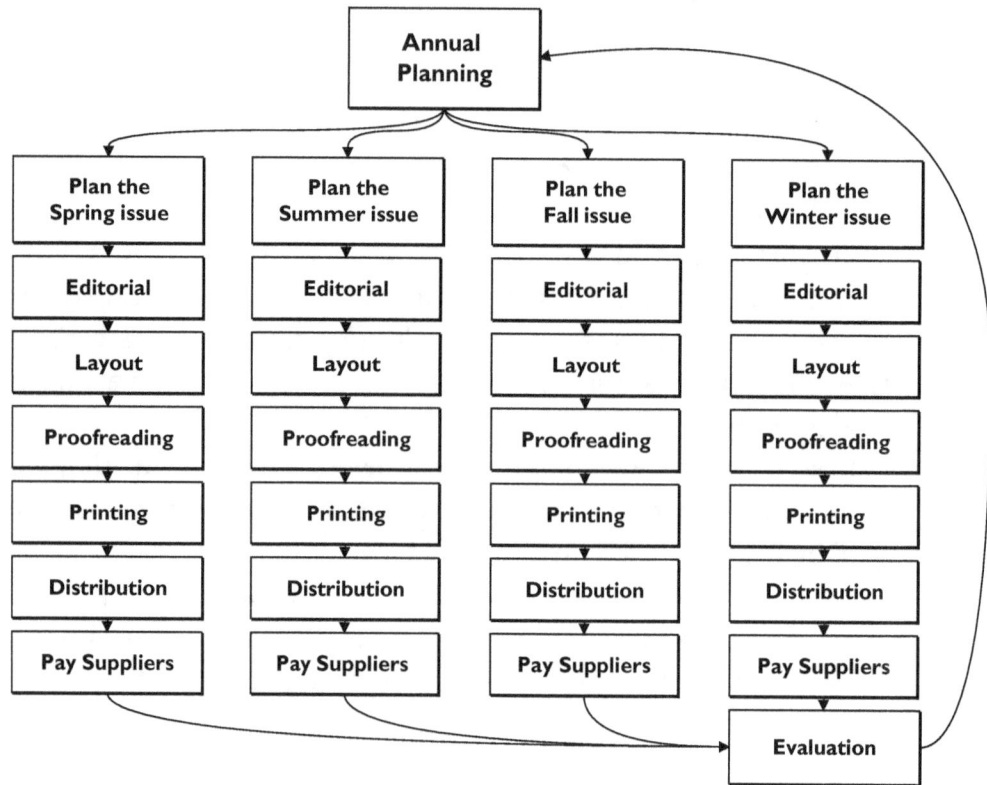

Figure 9–1

As indicated, a newsletter year begins with an annual plan (or a startup plan, if you're in the launch stage). The annual plan sets the general framework for the newsletter, with policies and guidelines.

Within that annual plan framework, the editorial board meets before work starts on each issue, and helps the editor shape it. This ensures the content and presentation of each issue are consistent with the strategy, tactics, and policies developed in departmental planning. The meeting before each issue is not held for the purpose of doing the editor's job, but through it, members of the board may provide support for the editor in a number of ways.

With planning for the issue completed, the editor and newsletter staff go to work on the tasks within their jurisdictions: editorial, layout, proofreading, printing, distribution, and paying suppliers. We consider each of these tasks in more detail in following sections.

At the end of the newsletter year members of the board evaluate how effective the newsletter has been. Results of the evaluation then feed into annual planning for the coming year.

With that overview in place, let's look at a more detailed list of activities. Again, remember that this is a generic list, or checklist. We hope that makes it more useful. It's presented from the perspective of an editor: In other words, an editor might use a list like this to ensure that all essential elements are completed, in the right order.

Planning

Annual
- ❏ Review the strategy and tactics (might include a review of Chapters 2 through 7 of this book)
- ❏ Review policy statements for each objective
- ❏ Review measures that track progress toward the objectives
- ❏ Prepare a generalized schedule for issues over the coming year, using standard time allotments for layout, printing, and distribution
- ❏ Prepare a budget for the coming year
- ❏ Allocate responsibilities and authority, as necessary

Each issue
- ❏ Decide on the goals for the issue
- ❏ Prepare a schedule for the issue, based on the generalized schedule prepared in the annual planning exercise
- ❏ Set the budget, and list anticipated exceptions for the issue
- ❏ Discuss the subjects and sources, and then make content decisions for the issue

Editorial management
- ❏ Prepare a style sheet, if one doesn't already exist
- ❏ Prepare and print a spelling worksheet (see Note 1 below)
- ❏ Prepare and print a grammar-checking worksheet (see Note 2 below)

- ❏ Prepare contributor guidelines
- ❏ Contact contributors and sources
- ❏ Make reminder contacts, as necessary
- ❏ Research and write articles, or edit contributions; take photos; create graphic materials
- ❏ Collect all articles, features, and text documents
- ❏ Put all text materials into one word processing document
- ❏ Check spelling, using a computerized spell checker
- ❏ Use grammar-checking software to check readability statistics:
  - Number of words in the document
  - Average number of words per sentence
  - Average number of letters per word
  - Proportion of passive verbs
  - Level of reading ease

(While these numbers will mean little the first time you list them, you will find they provide benchmarks after you've produced a number of issues. We intentionally don't include the checking of grammar usage by the software. You may add it if you find it helpful.)

- ❏ Create a footer, listing the volume and number or date of publication, and the version number of the draft
- ❏ Print a draft version of the document
- ❏ Proofread the copy, writing notes on the printed page
- ❏ Reopen the original word processing documents, and make changes based on the proofreading and readability levels
- ❏ Perform a second spelling check
- ❏ Perform a second readability check, if necessary
- ❏ Print a new version of the document
- ❏ Proofread the new version, and make revisions as necessary
- ❏ Obtain approvals:
  - Using the word processor, prepare a separate document for each article that needs to be checked (by a person who was the source for it; through an interview, for example)
  - Print a copy of each article
  - Prepare a cover page for each article, listing
    > The name of the person(s) who will check it
    > The editor's name and phone number
    > A brief note on the objective of the article
    > Directions for marking changes: for example, "Write on the page."

> The date by which the proofed article must be returned
> The date when the newsletter will be printed
> A place or procedure for requesting extra copies of the newsletter
> Other notes or comments, as required
- ❏ File the returned approvals

Layout Activities

- ❏ Prepare a rough layout of the newsletter on paper
- ❏ Select graphics and photos to illustrate articles
- ❏ Open a desktop publishing program (use a template, when possible, for consistency)
- ❏ Prepare the layout, using text and graphics
- ❏ Check each article or feature against the word processing document or other source for the following elements:
  - All text and headlines are included
  - The headlines are distinct from normal text and from each other
  - Articles that should continue on another page do continue there
  - *Continued on* and *Continued from* notices accompany articles that go on to another page
- ❏ Check each graphic for the following elements:
  - It will be legible when printed
  - Captions are in place, and adequately explain the graphic or photo
  - Graphics are linked to related articles, either by adjacent position or words
  - Each graphic is timely and relevant

Proofreading

- ❏ Print a proof copy of the newsletter
- ❏ Visually check the spelling and grammar
- ❏ Using a red pen, underline any facts or inferences that need to be checked
- ❏ Using a red pen, underline all names and sources, for checking
- ❏ Prepare a distribution cover page for the document, and add notes to it as follows:
  - List the proofreader to whom it is directed, or list the routing
  - Specify how each proofreader signs off
  - List the date by which the proof must be returned to the editor
  - Note any specific checks requested of individual proofreaders

- Write out any other special instructions
- ❏ List the date by which the distribution copy is to be returned
- ❏ After the proofs are returned, reopen the desktop publishing document and make the changes specified by proofreaders
- ❏ Recheck spelling
- ❏ Print two copies of the revised proof, and
  - File one copy with the docket
  - Provide one copy to the printer
- ❏ File the marked proof(s) in the docket

Printing

- ❏ For the printing service or company, prepare an information document that includes at least the following information:
  - The name of the newsletter and the organization publishing it
  - The name and version number of the desktop publishing software
  - A list of files transferred or supplied on diskette
  - The date submitted, and the date the printed copies should be delivered
  - The number of copies and colors
  - Notes on any scanning or pasting requirements
  - Any special instructions
  - The name and phone number of a contact person
  - A specification of what proofs to supply, and what other checks or confirmations are to be carried out before printing begins
  - Invoicing information
- ❏ Prepare a package for the printing company that includes
  - A copy of the information document (as described in the previous section)
  - Your laser- or inkjet-printed copy of the newsletter
  - A copy of the newsletter on diskette, or as transferred files, from the desktop publishing program
  - Copies of the fonts used in the document (you might check with your font vendor to ensure you won't violate the font-licensing agreement – it's normally not a problem)
  - Any other computer files the printing company requires
- ❏ After receiving a proof from the printing company, check
  - The nameplate, usually found at the top of Page 1
  - The date of publication or volume number
  - All headlines

- The legibility of graphics
- The captions for graphics
- All page numbers and page cross-references
- The text: check each page as an individual unit (do not move from page to page)
- All names and titles: make one pass on which you check only these
- End-of-article markers
- Articles that continue on other pages, for
  > *Continued on* and *Continued from* notices
  > Following-page headlines
  > Presence of all required text and absence of any wrongly-placed text, where articles break or continue

❏ Make notes on the proof as required
❏ Sign and return the proof

Distribution

❏ Update the list of recipients and locations
❏ Prepare special bundles for locations that require more than one copy
❏ Arrange delivery of individual copies and multiple-copy bundles

Payment of suppliers

❏ Review each invoice
❏ Place a copy of each invoice in the docket
❏ If there are expected variances from the budget, make a note or attach a note to the filed copy of the invoice
❏ If there are unexpected variances, determine the reasons and respond as required
❏ Also note any discrepancies in agreed delivery dates or scope of services or products delivered
❏ Prepare a brief report if significant changes are needed
❏ Authorize or make payments

Evaluation (through the process again, in reverse)

❏ Payment of suppliers:
- Did the suppliers perform as specified?
- Were external suppliers on budget?
- Were external suppliers paid on time?

- Did internal suppliers receive credits, recognition, or other acknowledgments?
❏ Distribution
  - Did everyone in the target audience(s) get copies?
  - Did people who asked for multiple copies get the number they requested?
❏ Printing
  - Did we provide all specifications, information, and materials that the printer required?
  - Did we provide them on time?
  - Did the quality of the printing meet expectations?
  - Was the printed product delivered on time?
  - Was the invoice for the amount quoted?
❏ Proofreading
  - Were there any mistakes or oversights that should have been caught?
  - Did each of the designated proofreaders check the proof and report back?
❏ Editorial and layout
  - Did the articles and graphics meet the guidelines set by the editorial board?
  - Did each element (text or graphic) serve the purpose for which it was intended and help achieve the objectives for this issue?
  - Were approvals obtained where required?
❏ Planning
  - Did this issue help achieve the newsletter's overall or long-term objectives?
  - Do we need to reconsider our objectives, or our lists of reader preferences and needs?
  - Are the measurements we use to track our progress adequate and appropriate?

Notes:
1. A spelling worksheet specifies the spelling of words that might be spelled differently by different authors. For example, Canadians sometimes use the British version of words like *humour* and *centre,* and sometimes the American versions, which are spelled *humor* and *center.* Similarly, variations in the use of technical language, or in the application of technical and lay terms, make a usage guide valuable.

2. A grammar-checking worksheet provides a list of specifications for important elements of the readability analysis, such as the proportion of passive verbs or a readability grade level. You may find it helpful to create a worksheet for the final results of each check, to ensure consistency over time.

Scheduling

By working through the process in reverse we get a framework for scheduling. To do this, we start with distribution, specifying what date we want readers to get the newsletter. With the date identified, we can work back through the newsletter process – allowing blocks of time for each set of tasks – to a starting date.

When preparing schedules, use working days, which normally means five days in each week, not seven. And if you're working with bi-monthly or quarterly newsletters, base your calculations on weeks, rather than the number of days per month. For example, in planning a quarterly newsletter, there will be 13 weeks between issues, and five working days per week, for a total of 65 working days. For a bi-monthly newsletter, divide 52 weeks by 6 issues, to get 8.6 weeks per issue. And multiplying 8.6 weeks by 5 working days gives us an average of 43 working days per issue.

Here's a sample schedule, using a quarterly newsletter as an example. Times (in days) are estimates, and refer to the number of days between starting and completing a task, not the amount of time needed to do the tasks. We began creating this schedule by setting a date for distribution of the completed newsletter: June 30th (Note that weekend days are not counted, as you can see in Printing which counts only 3 days between June 25 and June 30).

Task	Duration	Dates
Distribution		June 30
Printing	3 days	June 25 – June 30
Review printer's proof	2 days	June 23 – June 25
Printer prep time	5 days	June 18 – June 23
Final layout	2 days	June 16 – June 18
Reviews and approval	5 days	June 9 – June 16
First layout	3 days	June 4 – June 9
Editing and revisions	10 days	May 21 – June 4
Editorial Board review	5 days	May 14 – May 21
Research, writing, design	15 days	April 23 – May 14
Editor's planning	10 days	April 9 – April 23
Editorial Board meeting		April 9

According to our schedule, the editorial board should meet no later than April 9 to initiate this issue. And if it met a week earlier, on April 2, that would provide five buffer days for slack, days that might be needed by the time the issue is completed.

A table-type schedule such as the one above suits most purposes. But we can add another dimension to the schedule, so that it shows not only dates, but also who is doing what, and at which stage of the process. This is illustrated in Figure 9–2:

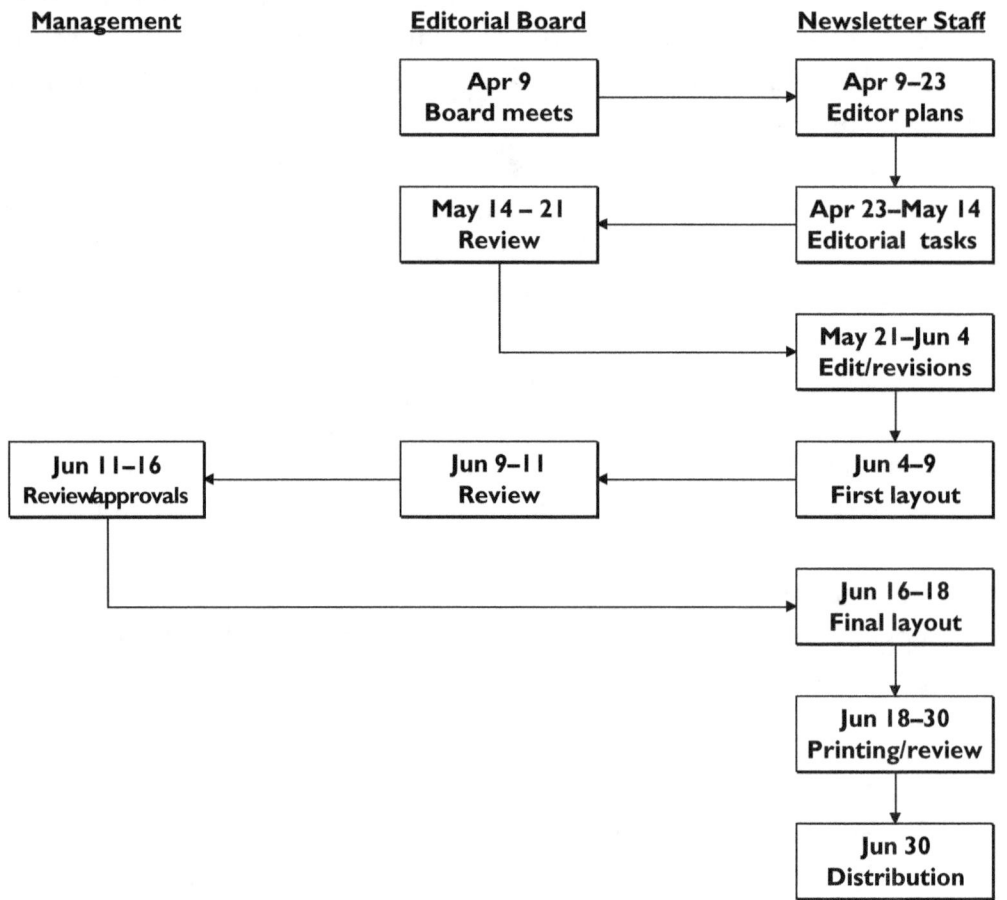

Figure 9–2

Of course, if only the staff (and not the board or management) actively prepares and puts together the newsletter, then a multi-dimensional schedule is less informative. In the example shown above, the editorial board is active.

Schedule killers

As someone who's published many newsletters, under many sets of circumstances, I should be good at getting them out on time. I should be, but I'm not. And I hope to be, but haven't succeeded yet.

On the positive side, while some of my newsletters are late, they do get out. And I know many people and organizations who've given up their newsletters altogether because they've been so late so often that it seemed there just wasn't any point in trying any more. There are many reasons why newsletters get delayed, and we'll take a look at a few of them here.

First, there's the fuzzy-focus problem. A newsletter launched without a proper sense of purpose is likely to be delayed because of changing priorities or lack of decisiveness. For example, work might be well underway on the content when the publisher begins to think that perhaps another subject might be better than the one now being developed. So, she starts again, from scratch, although she's already used up much of her buffer time, or even her operations time. And having changed the subject once, she may consider changing it again. Or, she may decide that the first subject was a better one after all. All of this leads us to emphasize the need for strategic and tactical clarity.

Another common cause of delay is the contributor who can't be rushed. Some publishers of marketing newsletters, for example, like to have clients or customers contribute articles or features. And of course, the publisher may want to start with one of his best clients, ones he wouldn't like to lose. This is a good idea, theoretically speaking, but if the client is late in submitting his contribution, there's not a lot the publisher can do. He can only request – he can't demand – that the client have the article ready by a certain date.

Similarly, the more contributors or suppliers involved, the greater the likelihood of delays: first, because miscues can occur when a project moves from person to person, and second, because others probably don't share your priorities. Almost all of us operate with many demands on our time, some more important than others. And while the newsletter may be at the top of your priority list, it may not be at the top of someone else's.

An obvious cause of delay is lack of planning. By planning before doing, we can anticipate the hurdles that may have to be cleared during the process. For example, if we know that we'll be mailing our newsletter during the Christmas season, we can expect delivery to take longer than at other times. In addition, planning allows us to give contributors and suppliers more time and flexibility. Of course, the further forward we plan, the less flexibility we have, and that, too, must be considered in the mix.

One answer to these sources of delay is simplicity. Consider *The Sovereign Report*, which has been on time through almost all of its nine years of publishing. It has a targeted audience, and the publisher knows the audience well. It has a clear purpose, which is to provide helpful marketing and managing information, which in turn is expected to help maintain a good relationship with readers. Only two people are involved in preparing the content (text only – there are usually no graphics), and layout is simply a matter of centering text on each page. Printing poses few difficulties because it's merely a matter of putting one color (black) on preprinted blank forms. And distribution is done in-house, using the company's own database of names and addresses. All in all, there are few of the challenges – and delays – that more complex or more ambitious newsletters face.

Chapter 10
Newsletter budgets

In this chapter...

If you've ever been involved in budgeting you'll know the frustration involved in trying to set figures without knowing the assumptions or objectives behind the line items.

This chapter deals with that problem. First, we set parameters and test our assumptions by reviewing the decisions and plans we worked on in the *Strategy* and *Tactics* sections of this book. Then, we adjust our figures to reflect those strategic and tactical decisions and plans.

With those issues settled, we go through budgeting on a line-by-line basis, starting with the four main types of expenses:

- Setup costs
- Development costs
- Direct per-issue costs
- Period costs

Having identified and quantified these costs, we can prepare reasonably accurate budgets:

- From setup and development costs, a startup budget
- From period costs, a period costs budget
- From direct per issue costs, a budget for individual issues

These budgets, in turn, can be used to create an annual budget. And finally, by dividing the total spending of the annual budget by the number of issues per year, we can create a full costs-per-issue budget.

Budgets: two questions

This chapter covers two major concerns, expressed in the following questions:
- How much should we spend?
- How much will it cost?

While these two questions may sound similar, they have very different meanings — and implications. The first question, "How much should we spend?" deals with issues that define the newsletter objectives. The second question, "How much will it cost?" deals with the administrative process of developing a budget – within the guidelines.

There's always a temptation to start with the second one first: to start writing down numbers on a piece of paper. But those of us who've done that know it can be a never-ending process. Go through, get finished, then question the assumptions and start over again.

If we deal with the strategic and tactical issues first, we should be able to approach the second part of the budgeting process with greater confidence – and do it just once.

"How much should we spend?"

The answer to this question reflects the kinds of decisions we made while going through the strategic and tactical issues in Chapters 1 through 7. Essentially, three criteria that affect budgets have emerged:
- How many pages?
- How often?
- How many copies?

These questions obviously indicate an emphasis on printed newsletters. Nevertheless, publishers of electronic newsletters can use the principles discussed here to develop specifications as well.

How many pages or words?

In considering the number of pages or words, publishers of electronic and printed newsletters take divergent courses.

For electronic newsletters, the question poses few budgeting challenges. Essentially, size doesn't matter, although e-mail messages over certain sizes, perhaps 30,000 characters, are converted from text to attachments. That reduces readership and leads to loss of subscribers.

Newsletters posted in HTML (Hypertext Markup Language) on Web sites do not suffer this constraint. However, if you publish long newsletters quite frequently, you might want to consider the storage costs imposed by your Internet Service Provider, although they will be a minimal expense.

For publishers of printed newsletters, size has an appreciable effect on costs. Printers base part of their fee on the amount of paper you use, and the amount of ink necessary to print each page (for more information on this subject, see *Fixed and Variable* costs in Chapter 14).

In addition, increments to page counts are large and costly. If you send your newsletter out to a printing company, the normal increments will be four pages. You publish 4 pages, 8 pages, 12 pages, and so on, to avoid paying for special paper sizes or folding.

While comparing the costs of electronic and printed newsletters, we might also introduce the issue of labor or time. Presumably, the same amount of time would be spent planning, researching, writing, and rewriting. From personal experience, I expect about the same amount of time to go into either desktop publishing (printed newsletters) and HTML coding (for electronic newsletters published on Web sites).

You also may find it helpful to review the presentation voices (Chapter 6). Some voices, such as *advise, challenge, consult, entertain,* and *empathize* require a relatively small amount of space; other voices such as *analyze, teach, envision, solve,* and *interpret* require relatively larger amounts of space.

With all these thoughts in mind, let's revisit the table we developed in Chapter 7 (electronic publishers can extrapolate into number of words by assuming 250 to 300 words per printed page):

	Change	Reinforce
1 Objective	2 pages	1 page
2 Objectives	4 pages	2 pages
3 Objectives	6 pages	3 pages
4 Objectives	8 pages	4 pages

Think of these guidelines as starting points for a discussion of your needs and intentions. As noted, our table shows various numbers, while printers normally deal in multiples of two and four pages.

If you didn't decide how many pages or words after reading Chapter 7, you should do it now.

How often?

Frequency, or how often you publish, depends on the willingness of readers to respond. A high degree of willingness allows you to publish less often, while a low degree requires more frequent publication.

From a budgeting perspective, publishers of printed newsletter must be more concerned about costs than electronic publishers. For example, each print issue requires prepress services by the printing company. In addition, if you mail enough newsletters to use a bulk mailing rate, you should factor that into your considerations.

Electronic newsletters, on the other hand, are relatively free of cost considerations. If you have a small list of recipients you can send the newsletter yourself, and a minimal amount your time will needed. If you have a large list, you'll probably distribute through an online mail management service. Generally, these providers charge on a monthly or annual basis, and within those periods you can send any number of newsletters without incurring extra costs. Similarly, you face few, if any, extra costs to posting a newsletter on a Web site.

For printed newsletters, frequency generally ranges from monthly to quarterly. For an electronic newsletter, the most common range seems to be from daily to monthly. And, given essentially non-existent distribution costs, Internet-based newsletters can be sent as a series of small documents, rather than one large one.

Again, we'll borrow guidelines from Chapter 7, with the qualification that you should determine the responsiveness of your readers and schedule accordingly:

	Electronic	Printed
Marketing newsletter	Weekly	Monthly
Employee newsletter	Monthly	Bi-monthly
Member newsletter	Monthly	Quarterly

How many copies?

If you publish an employee newsletter, calculating the size of your print run will be quite straightforward, with the number of copies roughly equal to the number of employees. To that you'll probably want to add an extra five or 10 percent for distribution to other stakeholders.

Member newsletter print runs also will be simple to figure if you distribute only to members. But of course, many associations and not-for-profits want to spread their messages not only to members and potential members, but also to the community, to influence opinion leaders and others. This just means that the publishers of membership newsletters face many of the same decisions that publishers of marketing newsletters face.

For marketing and customer newsletters, the distribution decisions are both more difficult and more important. In the end, though, the number of people who get the newsletter should be based on the scope of the objectives you want to achieve. Ambitious goals mean larger mailing lists; modest goals, smaller lists.

In the case of electronic newsletters, the number of copies has no direct bearing on cost, unless the number is extremely large. However, there are often costs associated with building up a list of subscribers, which may range from a few cents to several dollars per name.

How much will it cost?

Once we've defined the issues of frequency, page count, and number of copies, we can start working through the line-by-line process of building a budget.

Classification of costs

Working out the costs of a newsletter can be difficult. But a couple of techniques make it much easier and faster. One is the exercise we've just been through. The other is breaking down costs into a number of smaller pieces, rather than trying to estimate a complete figure in only one step. In addition, a budget is likely to be more accurate, and better understood, when approached on a line-by-line basis.

We start this process by classifying the different types of costs that might be encountered in a newsletter budget. Here's one breakdown that you may find useful:

1. Setup costs: the human and physical resources required to get started
2. Development costs: the planning and design needed to provide proper editorial and strategic foundations
3. Period costs: indirect costs that are incurred by the month or year, rather than per issue
4. Direct per-issue costs: direct costs incurred in preparing, printing, and distributing each issue

Figure 10–1 shows how these costs relate to each other (we'll discuss *amortization* and *annualization* later in the chapter), and are used to generate annual and full cost-per-issue budgets:

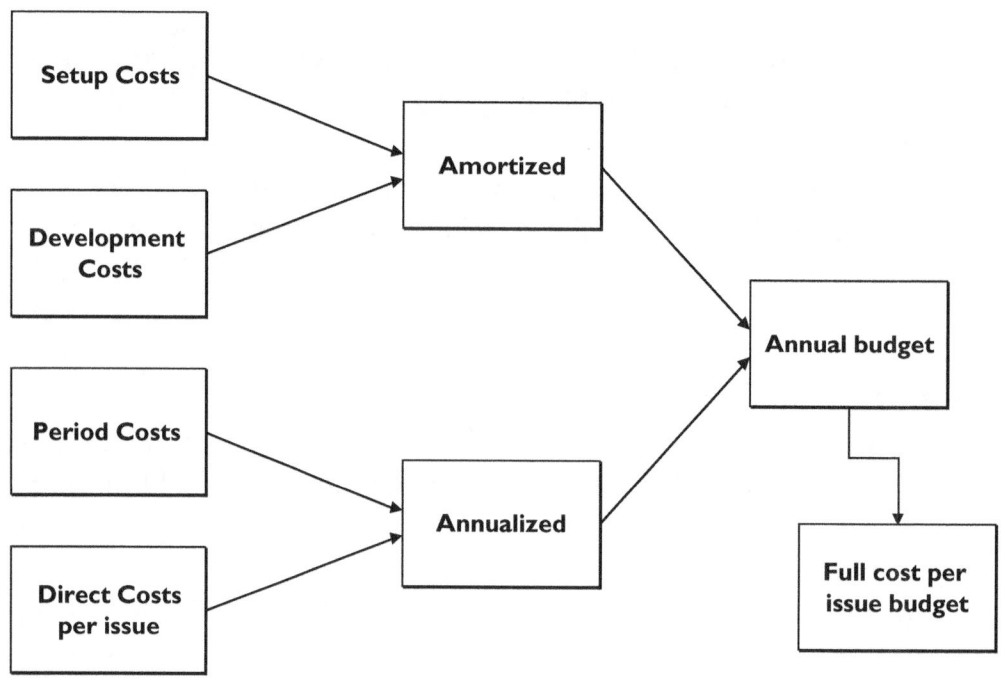

Figure 10-1

Setup and development costs

Setup costs include the expenses of recruiting, setting up an office, and buying equipment. Generally, these will be human resource costs for staffing and the costs of providing space and equipment for staff.

Setup costs

- Recruiting: If you use a current employee (or employees), assess the transfer costs, as well as training, retraining, documentation, and other expenses. If the position(s) will be filled by someone from outside, applicable costs might include those of advertising for candidates, screening and selecting a candidate, allocating additional salary and benefits, and covering extra taxes and levies.
- Training: This may involve sending staff to training courses, meeting with newsletter staff in other organizations for ideas and procedures, and meeting with senior staff for briefings or orientation.
- Office space: Calculate the share of total space and improvements now and in the near future. (Note: rent or its equivalent is covered under period costs.)
- Furniture, fixtures, telephones.
- Computer(s), printer, fax, and modem.

- Software, including word processor, desktop publishing program, database, and utility packages.
- Stationery and office supplies.
- Other: Add any other one-time costs you think will have to be covered.

Plan to amortize (spread) these costs over several years, to reflect their ongoing value. Usually, a period of three to five years covers the useful life span of such expenses.

Calculate the amortization by dividing the total amount from these lines by the number of years over which you want to spread the cost. That will give you an annual cost you can plug in to budgets. For example, let's suppose you want to spread the cost of $6,000.00 worth of computer hardware and software over three years:

```
Cost of equipment:      ..........$6,000.00
Divided by years of service .            3
Cost per year   .............$2,000.00
```

Development costs

The foundations of successful newsletters are laid long before the first word is written. Planning and design work undertaken before publishing begins are an excellent investment. Spend a lot of time (but not necessarily a lot of money) at this stage.

- Reader needs: How much will be spent to identify and define the needs of readers, as discussed in Chapters 3 and 13? Does the process include market research, an in-house survey, or just estimates?
- Objectives: Costs to be considered include evaluation of existing communication programs, research on organizational requirements, consultants' time, and evaluation of other newsletters.
- Editorial concepts: Develop plans that should satisfy or achieve the organizational objectives. Potential costs include editor's and publisher's time, management review and approval time, and perhaps consultants' fees.
- Design: Design of the front, back, and inside pages may require the services of an in-house designer or outside service. Whether internal or external, use the services of a professional graphic artist.
- Budgets and schedules: These require the time of the editor or publisher (to prepare them), and of management (to review and approve them).

Again, amortize these costs over several years, and calculate an annual amount to be added to your budgets.

Operating costs

Period costs

Period costs are not one-time expenses incurred in starting up the newsletter, nor are they associated with the costs of individual editions. Instead, they're characterized by their association with calendar periods such as months and years. Typical period costs include rent, utilities, and insurance. Often, these costs get billed to the organization as a whole, and portions are allocated to different functions or departments on the basis of space used or some other rationale. In other organizations, there is no allocation; the whole cost is simply a line in an overhead.

We annualize these costs to make them consistent with each other, and to avoid confusion in budgeting. To annualize a cost, multiply a monthly expense by 12, a quarterly expense by four, and so on. For example:

```
Telephone and fax (monthly)  . . . .$200.00
Multiply by 12 months . . . . . . . . .     12
Total annual cost . . . . . . . . . . . .$2,400.00
```

The annualized cost can now be plugged into your budgets.

Direct costs per issue

The main costs of producing a newsletter, and the most familiar, are the direct costs per issue. Each can be directly attributed to a specific issue of the newsletter. They include

Issue planning
- Editor's time
- Management time

Text
- Editor's time
- Research costs
- Writer time or fees

Graphics
- Editor's time
- Art or photo purchases

- Designer time or fees

Layout
- Desktop publishing services
- Outside services

Printing
- Liaison time
- Printing costs

Distribution
- Mailing costs
- Handling costs

Like setup costs, these are annualized. Multiply each cost or the sum of the costs by the number of issues per year.

The annual budget

The annual budget remains the basic financial document guiding development and production of newsletters. Prepare it using the figures developed in preceding sections, or by using your own estimates for each category.

At this point you may discover the value of amortizing and annualizing. It means you're working with consistent numbers across the board. Every cost item will be listed as the cost for one year, which makes preparation of the annual budget quick and easy.

The lines in your annual budget will look something like this:
- Setup costs (annualized)
- Development costs (annualized)
- Period costs (annualized)
- Direct costs per issue, multiplied by the number of issues per year

For example:

Setup costs (one year's amortization)	$1,000
Development costs (one year's amortization)	200
Period costs (annualized)	1,000
Direct cost-per-issue $1,000	
Multiplied by number of issues .....<u>4</u>	
Direct costs-per-issue (annualized)	<u>4,000</u>
Total annual budget	$6,200

Full cost-per-issue budget

From the annual budget, it's a quick step to figure out the full costs per issue. Simply take the total annual budget, and divide by the number of issues per year. That will include both direct and indirect costs, such as a portion of the startup costs (setup and development) and period costs.

For example:

```
Annual budget . . . . . . . . . . . . . . . . . . . . .$6,200
Divided by number of issues . . . . . . . . . . . . . .4
Full cost-per-issue . . . . . . . . . . . . . . . . . .$1,550
```

When we compare the full cost per issue with the direct cost per issue, we see that while the direct costs amounted to $1,000 per issue, the other costs (including setup, development, and period costs) added another $550 per issue to our total costs.

Chapter 11
Media relations

In this chapter...

Using your newsletter as a media relations tool offers a number of potential benefits:
- Extending your reach or influence beyond targeted readers
- Increasing your credibility and influence with targeted readers
- Added impact on targeted readers

To catch the interest of the mass media, though, you must understand and meet their needs. These media compete for readers, viewers, and listeners; they do it by finding and delivering features that serve the needs of their audiences for entertainment or information.

For media people, a good article includes one or more of these characteristics:
- Widespread interest
- Information that is new or unique
- Some dramatic quality
- Appropriate timing

While newsletters can be sent to the media on their own, your efforts will be more effective if you attach a personalized note to the newsletter. The note should highlight articles or other features that address the needs of individual reporters and editors.

Do not use your newsletter to deliver breaking, or urgent, news. Important bulletins should be sent by courier or electronically, with appropriate covering information.

Leveraging the value of your newsletter

One way to increase the impact of your newsletter is to use it as a media relations tool. You might want to look at media relations as a way of gaining an extra benefit for little added cost.

Media relations refers to the practice of getting or influencing coverage in the mass media – newspapers, magazines, radio stations, television stations, and now electronic media – to sell your product or service, or to advocate your cause.

All of this assumes you are undertaking media relations for the sake of the organization, not to promote just the newsletter. The newsletter becomes an additional tool for use by the person responsible for building or maintaining relationships with the media. It also assumes the newsletter is aligned and integrated with the objectives and operations of the organization as whole.

Not every organization wants media attention, of course, but some want a good relationship with the mass media because they need publicity or attention. Others have a reluctant relationship, and try to manage or minimize their exposure in the media. In either case, a newsletter used for media relations may be useful.

In this chapter, we'll consider some of the basics involved in media relations, and relate them to newsletters. Most of what we talk about makes direct reference to news departments, but many of the same things can be said about specialty departments. These areas, such as sports, gardening, entertainment, business, and fashion, deal with specialized audiences within the broader audience, or deal with them as separate audiences. The same rules apply, so even if your newsletter doesn't deal with public affairs, it still may interest editors and reporters in those departments.

The benefits

Circulation

Newsletters work best when directed to niche audiences. With controlled circulation, they provide specific information to a targeted group of readers. There are times, though, when the organization benefits from a wider distribution of its news, as indicated in Figure 11–1.

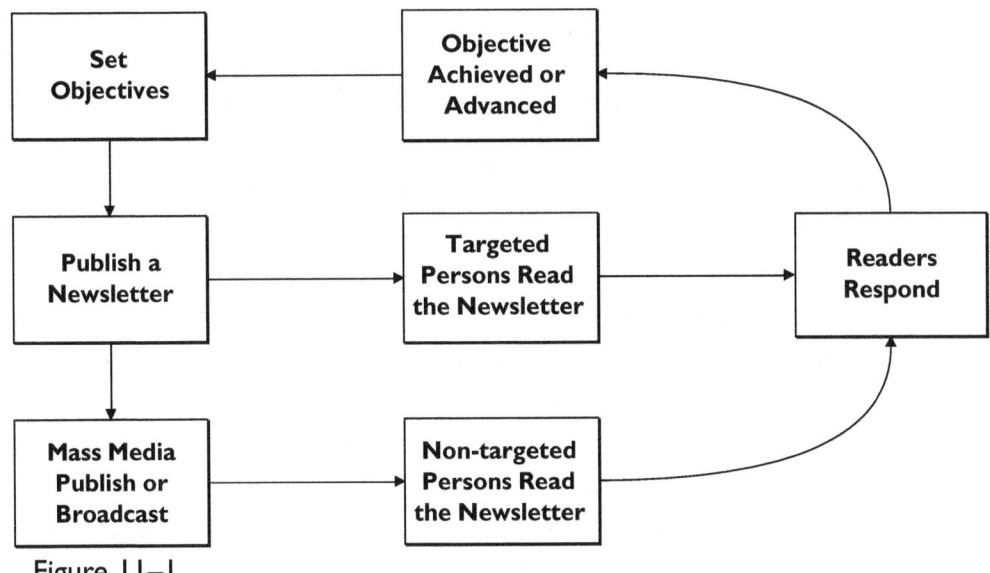

Figure 11-1

Two types of supplementary circulation are of interest when we use a newsletter for media relations. One is broad circulation to the mass media, which is especially important when an organization wants public support or widespread awareness. The other is controlled circulation to trade and special interest media, which can spread your article within an industry or an area of interest.

Perceived credibility

The mass media, which depend on continuing reader or viewer interest, generally have more perceived credibility than newsletters. This is, of course, perceived credibility and the content of mass media is not necessarily more accurate or objective than that of a newsletter.

Nevertheless, these perceptions might aid your newsletter. If the media reference or use articles from your newsletter, your credibility increases. If you do get coverage, be sure to cite it in the next issue of your newsletter.

Added impact

The mass media can increase your influence on the readers your newsletter has targeted. This can happen in two ways.

First, repetition of your message in other media provides more exposures (repetition), which should increase the impact. And the mass media will probably rewrite your message, which means that targeted readers will be exposed to it in a different form. Second, the media will probably put the message into a different environment, which means your readers will see it in relation to different products or issues.

Setting context

The benefits we've examined so far relate to immediate effects. But there is another type of benefit – setting context – that should be considered as well. Setting context is using your newsletter to develop relationships with editors and reporters. As the word *develop* suggests, this involves a longer-term perspective.

Backgrounding, interpreting, and providing *contact information* are three important ways of providing context and developing relationships.

Backgrounding means offering information that helps editors prepare accurate articles. Editors may create a file for your background information documents, or merely make mental notes about you and your organization. Whatever the case, they will be able to write more accurately about your organization or the issues it champions if they know more about you than is contained in a single issue of your newsletter.

Backgrounding also might be seen as setting context for your big announcements in the future. If reporters prepare an article on a subject that's not immediately familiar to their audiences, they'll try to put it into some sort of context. By explaining the issue in advance, you increase the likelihood that reporters will use your framework.

Interpreting refers to the process of explaining a story, or your side of it, with emphasis on the important points and their implications as you see them. High-profile negotiations, for example, attract media attention, and a newsletter can explain or support controversial positions. Cynics refer to this process as spin doctoring.

Again, this can be useful in setting the stage for future news. In this case, it's a matter of setting your side of the article within the broader framework you choose.

Contact information provides basic information that the media find useful in reaching or describing your organization, such as:
- Its full and proper name
- Business address, phone, and fax numbers
- The names and titles of senior managers or elected officers
- Organizational details, such as the number of employees or members
- The name of a media contact person for the organization
- The stock symbol for public companies
- Statistical information about your industry or sector

Use your front page, back page, or editorial information column to provide at least some of this basic information. While the information may seem obvious or well known, it probably doesn't seem so simple or easy for a reporter, especially one who's in a hurry.

On the record
In addition to background information, editors like to have some quotable information, which is called *on the record* material. That is, they look for previously published quotations or facts to help develop their articles.

Newsletters often quote officers or managers of their organizations, and because senior persons made those statements publicly (in the newsletter), a reporter can cite them with reasonable confidence.

A word of caution
Many of the advantages or benefits listed here might well be looked at another way, and be considered problems or hazards. One of the reasons for publishing a newsletter is to maintain control over such things as context and timing, and you have no control (or little control) over the way the mass media use the material you provide. Because of this lack of control, many organizations not only ignore the mass media, but even go out of their way to avoid attracting their attention.

Getting mass media attention
The key to getting media attention is to understand the needs of reporters and editors, as well as some basic principles of the media business, then to work methodically to meet those needs.

News departments in newspapers and broadcast stations compete with each other, and often compete fiercely, for the attention of readers, viewers, and listeners. The winners of this competition, those that build the biggest audiences or those that deliver specific audiences, get the biggest share of advertising revenues.

This competition to attract audiences centers on the choice of content and its presentation. Out of the literally thousands of subjects and articles available on any given day, editors select those few that they think will be most relevant to the largest number of people in their audience. And those pursuing niche markets will select articles that appeal to as many readers or viewers as possible within those markets. To get coverage, then, you need to show that your article is not only relevant, but also appeals to the audiences the media serve.

Now, you may do everything right, and have what appears to be a good subject, but still not get any coverage in the mass media. Don't be surprised or disappointed. Although the issues may seem critical to you, editors may feel (rightly or wrongly) that only a limited portion of their audience would be interested. This is especially true among the major media, where there are many potential subjects, and competition for media attention is extensive.

In many cases, you may be further ahead to concentrate on smaller, more focused media. These might include a newspaper that serves one area of a city rather than the whole city, a specialty magazine rather than a mass market magazine, or perhaps other newsletters that could copy or rewrite your content in exchange for a byline or other recognition. The same holds for specialty media, which we address later in this chapter.

Note, too, that editors and reporters of the major media will be more likely than those of smaller publications to view newsletters as promoting the interests of a particular group, and therefore not credible. This underlines the need to understand and address the needs of the media you target.

What makes a good article?

There are several characteristics of a good news article, as summarized in Figure 11–2.

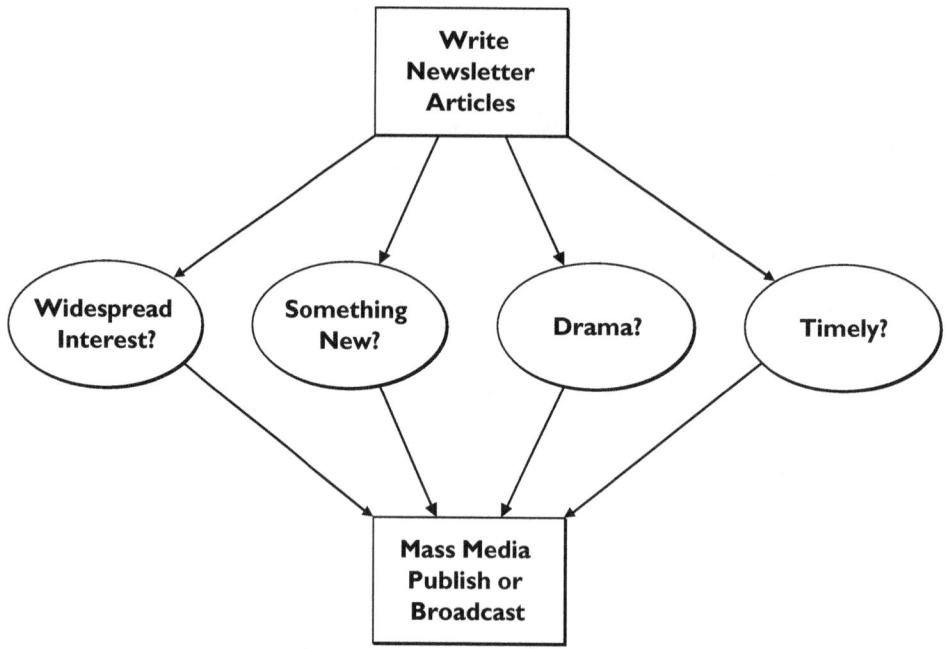

Figure 11–2

One characteristic is *widespread interest*, which means relevance to many members of a mass media audience. For example, political articles enjoy popularity with the media because many people are affected, directly or indirectly, by government action or decisions.

Reporters and editors use informal relevance filters, such as those discussed for newsletters in Chapter 5. Obviously, their filters will be somewhat coarser, because they have more diverse audiences. However, the same general principle applies – there must be some link between the message and the audience.

Something new. Even if the article is clearly important, editors question whether it presents anything new. Does it provide new facts or new opinions from a knowledgeable source, or introduce a new angle to an old article? Watch the evolution of any prominent, ongoing article in the news, and you will see that something new or different is added on each succeeding day.

Drama. Editors like articles with some dramatic aspect because that increases attention, and increased attention keeps the audience from changing channels or putting down newspapers. Again, political articles often satisfy this need in the media, as do articles from the police and courts.

Timeliness. The media like seasonal articles, such as gardening in the spring and the plight of the poor at Christmas. But timeliness also refers to public consciousness of broader issues. For example, economic issues get extra attention during recessions.

Keep in mind that editors in the mass media face many of the same challenges as you do. While not directly concerned with influencing the behavior of their audiences, they do need to deliver an audience that advertisers want to reach and want to influence. Without satisfied advertisers, no mass media organization can exist for long.

Determining their priorities

If media attention is important, target specific media and find out their priorities. The best way? Phone the editor or assignment director. Most will tell you what they want or need; indeed, many editors know they can get a competitive edge by building a broad network of volunteer contributors who call with tips and ideas.

Another approach is to monitor publications or broadcasts regularly until you have a good sense of their priorities. Since the articles that editors consider most important get the greatest prominence, don't evaluate every article in a newspaper or newscast. Look at the front pages of a newspaper, or consider the first few articles in a radio or television newscast. Evaluate each according to the criteria listed above and any other criteria that seem appropriate to you. But remember that emphasis may change from day to day, so you may need to monitor a medium for some time before any pattern appears, if it ever does.

Doing it

Now that we've considered the benefits and customers of our media relations efforts, we can discuss execution in more detail.

Send the newsletter

The simplest and most common approach is to put the appropriate media people on the newsletter mailing list. That means they automatically get a copy of the newsletter whenever it's sent to your targeted readers.

Effectiveness may be increased, though, by keeping the media list separate, and personalizing each mailing. That could involve a personalized letter, one which points out relevant articles or features, or perhaps provides some context for the editor's benefit.

Unless you and your organization are very well known, identify yourself and your organization, and point out your connection to the article. If you have a new angle to a current subject in the news, draw that to the editor's attention. Most editors deal with an overwhelming flow of fact, opinion, and other information every day. They appreciate a concise note alerting them to feature opportunities.

Telephone calls

While most editors will probably appreciate receiving your newsletter, they probably won't want you to call after delivery to see whether anything from it will be used. Editors can read or scan your newsletter at any time they choose, while phone calls may arrive when they're busy or focused on something else.

It is reasonably acceptable, though, to call before sending a newsletter for the first time. In that case, you'll be asking the editor if she would like to be on your mailing list, and the call also offers you an opportunity to find out about the editor's priorities and preferences, so you can target your mailings.

Timing

You can also gain effectiveness by controlling the timing of your mailings. Although they're always looking for news that serves their audience, news reporters and editors have slow news days and busy news days. On busy news days, your newsletter probably won't get much more than a glance. On a slow day (or in a slow season), your article may get full attention, whether as an article in itself, or as the basis for something developed in the newsroom.

That's the type of opportunity we're looking for in media relations. Of course, if your newsletter deals with issues that make the news on a regular basis, you may have opportunities on busy days as well. If your newsletter's content relates to an emerging story, it may be considered more thoroughly.

What's a slow time? For the answer to that, you'll have to contact each editor individually. For some, there are no slow days, and for others, too many days seem slow.

Breaking news

A newsletter should not be used to send breaking news, which might be defined as news that is time-sensitive or of immediate interest. Since newsletters rarely share the time-sensitivity of conventional media, mass media editors often assume mailed newsletters contain old news. Radio stations, newspapers, and television stations expect breaking news articles to arrive by e-mail, hand, courier, telephone, or fax.

A newsletter that does contain breaking news should be sent by courier or electronically, with a personalized note. That note should clearly outline the article, point out the news element, offer supporting evidence if necessary, and provide full contact information.

Again, this is a case where a phone call is appropriate. Give the editor a brief outline of the article, connect it with other news (context) if that's appropriate, and provide contact information that can be used for follow up. And if the editor wishes to pursue the idea, you can fax or forward newsletters that provide useful background or interpretive information.

Specialty media

Much of what we've just discussed refers to the mass media such as newspapers and broadcast stations. Dealing with specialty media, such as trade magazines, will be somewhat different, depending of course on the nature of the media you're trying to reach. Breaking news will be less of a concern, but depth of coverage will be important.

Specialty media, by definition, have audiences with something in common. Readers share something, and you need to address that something – in depth – for your media relations in this sector to be effective.

If, for example, it's an industry publication and your organization is part of that industry, then you're off to a good start. It's not like a mass media environment where you'll be competing with hundreds, if not thousands, of other organizations for attention. Here, you belong to a smaller, better-defined community.

That means it's more likely your material will be read, and its contents scrutinized. So, your covering letter should contain less self-promotion, and more colleague-to-colleague discussion. Obviously, not only the tone of the note will be different, but also the content.

Mailing list management

Keep your media mailing list distinct from the regular newsletter distribution list. This can be done by using a completely separate database, or by using a flagging option on your main database.

Whatever option you choose, consider the information in each edition of the newsletter in light of each media outlet. Write personalized notes to editors wherever appropriate, and make your own senior officials aware that reporters may be contacting them for comments and quotes. And use e-mail, fax, or a courier to distribute any newsletter that contains urgent news. Timing counts.

Chapter 12
Generating article ideas

In this chapter...

Several sources of article ideas, and methods for finding them, come out of this chapter. But before looking at them we review the framework for content developed in Chapter 5, where we asked the question, "What should we write about?"

What we should write about are subjects that fit within the shared environment. In other words, subjects that address the interests of both the reader and the publisher, and about which readers believe the publisher has above average knowledge, experience, or expertise.

In generating article ideas that fit these criteria, there are two general directions we can take:

- Provide unique information that is not available elsewhere.
- Provide condensed or expanded information, depending on the source and on reader needs.

Unique information usually comes from an organization's stakeholders, including managers, employees, suppliers, customers, and shareholders or owners.

Condensed or expanded information comes from other media and publications, including internal documents, industry reports, magazines and periodicals, and books.

Finally, we offer a list of forty sources and resources that you can tap to generate articles or article ideas.

When inertia sets in

If you've been part of an editorial board, or if you've managed a publication, you know the sort of trajectory that article ideas take. When a publication begins, all sorts of ideas come pouring in. There is lots of enthusiasm, but it doesn't last. So, what looked like a unending stream of article ideas begins to taper off, and the curve points downward very quickly. Soon, coming up with content ideas for every issue of the publication becomes a challenge.

In this chapter, we offer some ideas for systematically developing article ideas. But before going on to those ideas, let's review the framework we created for newsletter content in Chapter 5.

The shared environment

An effective newsletter, we've argued, does two important things – at the same time: It provides an opportunity to influence the attitudes or behaviors of readers as the publisher wishes, and it helps readers achieve their goals.

Subjects that meet these two criteria are deemed to be within the shared environment, as shown earlier in Figure 5–1.

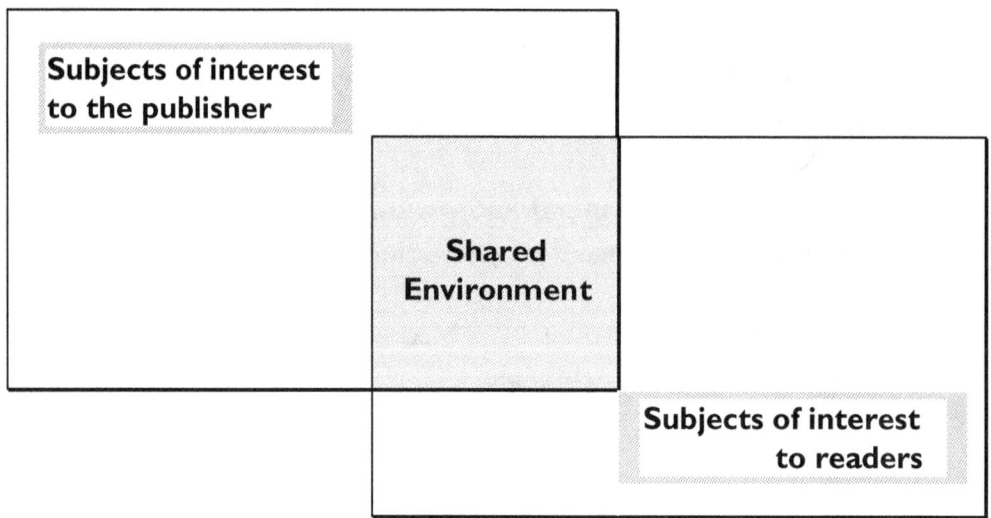

Figure 5–1

For an employee newsletter, anything that affects the company or organization affects both employees and management. In the case of a marketing newsletter, the shared environment includes the products that link the sellers and buyers. And for a membership newsletter, it's likely to be the cause or concern that brings members together.

Two tests for the shared environment are the relevance and credibility of the subject matter. First, would you rate the subject as relevant to both the reader and the publisher? Will both be affected if this subject is covered or not covered?

The second test is that of credibility. In what areas do your readers consider you to have expertise and experience? If they're not likely to perceive you as credible on the issue, then that issue probably falls outside the boundaries of the shared environment.

Getting more specific

Now that we've reviewed the framework for content, we can be more specific. But we also want to be systematic, so we have a process we can turn to repeatedly, rather than just a list that would be exhausted after a certain number of uses.

Later in this chapter you'll find a list of immediate sources and resources, but first let's set up our system. The system springs from the two reasons why newsletters are read by targeted readers: either the newsletters offer unique sources of information, or condensed or expanded information.

A unique source

In this era of specialization and fragmentation, every organization becomes a unique source of information. Some generate more than others, but all organizations, and the people associated with them, produce at least some information that cannot be found elsewhere.

Consider the five general constituencies that affect, or are affected by, an organization:
1. Employees, managers, committees, shareholders and owners
2. Customers, users, and members
3. Suppliers, contractors, and partners
4. The industry or sector
5. The public

Each set of stakeholders, except perhaps the last, possesses some unique knowledge or information that might help readers of a marketing, employee, or membership newsletter. To take the first constituency as an example, employees have front-line experience with products, services, and processes. Managers see how various processes fit together. Committees often deal with issues that overlap among processes. And shareholders or owners see how well a business uses its resources, especially in comparison with other firms.

Out of this brief list of five broad constituencies we can see a number of emerging article possibilities. We can use each of the sources individually, or we can use them in combination with each other. There are other benefits from using these sources – any articles we develop using them are likely to be both relevant and credible. Further, simply canvassing these sources on a regular basis may produce leads to other articles you might not have discovered otherwise.

In Chapter 5 we talked about micro and macro approaches to content, with macro referring to the interaction between the organization and the environment within which it operates. That interaction can be a rich source of new information for all types of newsletters. Micro refers to people, events, and processes within the organization itself. Generally, we expect the micro approach to help us find unique story ideas, and the macro approach to provide sources for condensation or expansion.

Condensation or expansion of information

Condensation and expansion of information are two common functions of newsletters. Condensation involves taking a deep or complex subject and boiling it down to its most basic elements. This allows readers to get at least a glimpse of a subject that might be too extensive or intimidating otherwise.

Expansion is the idea of building on and exploring a core idea. Health and safety issues are often treated this way, as managers take concisely written rules and expand on them so they will have context and mean more to the employees who work with them.

Some sources of information that can be compressed or expanded include

- Internal documents such as group insurance rules; descriptions of product features; health and safety documents; and organizational policy statements
- Trade magazines and subscription newsletters dealing with the industry
- General news and business magazines
- Books

Internal documents, policies, and forms in many organizations are concisely written – so concisely that only a person with a legal education can understand what they mean. The design of forms also can cause problems for members, employees, and customers, and a newsletter can explain, for instance, how to fill in the troublesome sections.

Trade magazines provide an ongoing stream of reports about critical issues affecting any industry. From these publications you can build a list of issues and consider each of them from the vantage point of your organization.

General news and business magazines are another source of ideas for articles. Again, it's less a matter of looking for direct applications than of looking for spin-offs and innovative approaches. Start in a library, then take out subscriptions after you've discovered the most useful sources.

Books can be approached from several directions. One is to simply list books that might interest readers, another is to publish excerpts (after getting permission from the publisher), and a third is to review them. Reviews are particularly valuable, because the nature of reviews permits you to evaluate books in relation to anything you choose, including your organization.

Whichever of these approaches you select, remember that you can use them as sources in themselves, and you also can use them as a stimulus to something else. Reprinting magazine and newspaper articles is also a valid option, and one that shouldn't be overlooked. Make a note of any article you come across that is well written, addresses the right issues, and is the right length.

But be sure you get permission to reprint. It was once safe to assume a reasonable number of words could be excerpted and quoted without permission. That assumption is no longer safe. Always check with the publisher or author; it's a relatively simple process – just create a form letter or two – and could prevent a lot of trouble later.

Condensation of your sources may mean rewriting them to capture the essence and leaving the rest behind. But it also might mean using a quotation that gives a flash of insight.

Expansion means elaborating on an idea in a way that appeals to readers in your target audience. Sometimes, an article can be both condensation and expansion. Consider a book review, which is a condensation for those who have read the book, and an expansion for those who have not.

List of sources and resources

Now, here's a list of 40 sources you may find helpful in developing content for your newsletter. While this section may be most appropriately in the domain of the editor, many editors ask their editorial boards for ideas and article suggestions, so this list may be relevant to managers as well as editors.

Annual reports

The annual (and quarterly) reports of your company, as well as those of your competitors and suppliers can all be sources. Consider both the financial results and management's discussion of the reasons for the results.

Associations
Various kinds of associations, from trade groups to volunteer coordination centers, report to their members regularly. Their reports have special value since they deal with issues familiar to or of concern to your readers.

Book reviews
These are a staple of periodicals, but don't hesitate to take a new approach to them. For example, you might review old books rather than new books, or you could review book reviews written by others. You can review something offbeat, such as a comic book, or excerpt passages from a book and make them the basis for something entirely different, such as a contest.

Calendar of events
Posting information about coming events can be a regular feature. Build on this by providing information or a form that explains how readers can add events to the calendar.

Cartoons
Cartoons are an old standard, but often hackneyed, especially if photocopied from other publications (which could involve copyright violations) or expressing a sentiment expressed too often before. Look for in-house and aspiring professional cartoonists, or buy cartoons from a syndication service.

Catalogs
These are a wildcard source, but given the vast variety of catalogs now appearing in mailboxes everywhere, they offer some new possibilities: absurd novelty items, new technology, and changing styles in everything from clothing to kitchen appliances.

Changes
Newsletters frequently contain explanations for changes. One helpful tactic is to explain the context within which the change was made.

Committees
Committees and their reports can have a big impact. To develop articles, look for long-term implications or consequences of committee decisions, as well as the basic news. Explain how the committee reached its conclusions, and perhaps quote the committee's sources of information and advice.

Competitors
What do your competitors have to say? Where are they advertising, and what do they say in their advertising? This may not be appropriate for marketing newsletters, but it could have a place in employee newsletters.

Compilations
If space is a problem, consider a piece that summarizes or uses excerpts from a number of articles. This is popular in newspapers and magazines at the end of the year: *The Year in Review,* for example.

Contests
Contests can serve several functions, and one of the more important among them is to encourage reader participation and comments. They can solicit prospective customers – "You could win a trip for two if your name is drawn" – and they can be educational, as well.

Crossword puzzles and crossword software
Crossword puzzles used to be limited to the generic puzzles from syndication services. But now you can use crossword puzzle software to create puzzles specifically for your organization, using words that mean something (or should mean something) to your readers.

Customers
Go beyond the usual endorsements and testimonials; ask customers to write articles based on their unique expertise or knowledge. Or write about their special achievements, locations, or clients.

Elaboration and sidebars
Take one idea from an article in your newsletter or other source, and elaborate on it. Watch for the sidebar technique in other print publications – you can identify them because they're set in different-colored or gray boxes, separate from but adjacent to the main article.

Employees
The employees are an obvious source for an employee newsletter, but they're also relevant for all other types of newsletters. Ask them to bring a unique angle to an article by developing it from their own experiences.

Excerpts and reprints
These provide good content for newsletters, either as independent subjects, or to supplement an article of your own. Often, excerpts are valuable because the writers who created them were able to describe their subjects in effective ways. (See **Rewrites** for another approach to using the words of others.)

Government reports
Many sources of government information exist, but you should try to get on the mailing lists of officials and agencies that deal with issues of concern to your organization. Also browse government reports for starting points to original articles of your own.

In-house experts
Interview people with special knowledge, skills, or expertise. Then write something or get them to write something for you. Watch for incidental opportunities, such as getting people who work in an internal finance function to write about income tax strategies.

Internet
The Internet, and particularly the World Wide Web section of it, can do triple duty. First, it's a source of information that can lead to articles, features, or graphic images; second, it's a tool for communication (through e-mail and online conferencing); and third, it's a subject in itself (You can write articles about how your customers are using it, for example).

Line art
With the proliferation of desktop publishing (DTP), more and more line art has become available. To find sources, look through computer and DTP magazines, call software retailers, or use the search engines on the Internet (try searching for "clip art").

Lists
Lists are very popular among readers, especially if they do some form of ranking. Magazine publishers report that lists such as the *Fastest Growing*, *Ten Largest*, and *Top 100* lists produce best-selling editions.

Magazines
Once a month, spend a couple of hours browsing in a library that has a broad collection of periodicals. You should be able to find articles to summarize and

ideas for articles of your own. Even browsing through the Tables of Contents of relevant periodicals can be helpful.

Managers

The letter from the president is an institution in many newsletters, but give some thought as well to insights available from others. Can the personnel manager offer some ideas on career trends? Can the safety director prepare an annual list of the ten most common mistakes that lead to injuries?

New products

Pay attention not only to the new products or services your organization creates or delivers, but also to the new products of other organizations that can help your readers accomplish something. Software reviews come to mind as an example.

Photos

Newsletters that deal with technical or abstract issues can increase reader appeal by adding photos of people. Avoid head-and-shoulders shots: Use photos of the whole person doing something, and preferably doing something with other people.

Puzzle books

While you can't just lift a puzzle, clues and all, from a book of puzzles, you could use it as a guide to creating your own. Puzzles provide a way of getting readers to participate in the newsletter and to build loyalty. Careful selection of puzzle types and clues can make puzzles a learning experience as well as entertainment.

Reader feedback

Letters to the editor are a traditional staple, but other possibilities exist. They include forums based on reader responses to a statement or challenge, and the results of reader surveys. Such surveys can be about the newsletter, or about any topic within your shared environment.

Reader turnover

A subject once covered does not need to be forgotten forever. If the readership of your newsletter changes over time you can, and perhaps should, repeat articles from the past. These repeats don't need to be redundant to readers who saw the original articles. Freshen them up by rewriting, or with new headlines and examples.

Research reports
Whether technological or social, research reports have become increasingly common. They make good newsletter articles when summarized, localized with the reaction of people in your organization, and accompanied by comments about the findings.

Retrospectives
First, collect a group of articles on a particular subject (from your newsletter or other publication) over the past year or few years. Then, look for changes over time that can be illustrated with references to those articles. For example, you might consider how a specific technology has evolved.

Revisit previous articles
As you complete an article for the newsletter, think about the possibilities for following up. For example, if the article is about a new computer system, revisit the article in a year, to find out how it performed. Don't forget to put copies of current articles in a future reference file.

Rewrites
One way to use the ideas of others is to print excerpts of their articles. Another is to rewrite their stories, creating your own article by describing their ideas in your own words. This offers several advantages: bringing in new ideas, condensing information, and putting ideas into a more relevant context. When you do this, be sure to acknowledge the source article and publication.

Shareholders and owners
If your company is privately owned and the owner can write well, her thoughts on the company's direction can be illuminating. Alternatively, she could write about industry trends, rather than about the company (See also **Annual reports**). If your company is publicly owned, perhaps the chairman could be asked to write something, or could be interviewed.

Spin-off articles
A variation on rewrites, spin-off articles allow us to localize an article, to introduce a new direction, or to consider new facts. The article starts with the central point of the original article, then goes on to develop that idea based on

your particular interest. If you're producing an electronic newsletter, you can hyperlink the original article and the spin-off article to each other.

Suppliers

Marketing newsletters, in particular, should consider contributions by suppliers. They can provide new insight into the *whys* and the *hows* of product performance. They can also provide warnings about coming changes and how such changes will affect product features.

Syndication services

These services can be useful, although most only offer very generalized articles, opinion pieces, and artwork. Nevertheless, if filling pages is a problem with every issue, then consider them. Check writers' and publishers' materials in your library to find lists of syndication services.

Trade associations

These are a very good source for newsletters, since they deal with relevant issues for companies. In addition to the editorial material you can get from a trade association, you can report on the fortunes of the association itself. Your readers may be interested in knowing whether it is growing or shrinking, for example. Also, you can interview officers or staff of the association on appropriate issues.

Trade periodicals

Again, examine more than just the editorial content. Who is advertising, and what are they advertising? Is the amount of advertising content rising or falling? Has the editorial direction changed? Is circulation up – or down?

Unions

Possibilities include interviews with union representatives and articles in union publications. For employee newsletters, there will be obvious relevance; for marketing newsletters, articles about the labor climate may be relevant to readers.

Year end and anniversaries

Go through back issues for the previous year and look for unexpected changes, exciting developments, milestones, and other events that help readers put the preceding 12 months into some kind of context.

Section 4: Evaluation

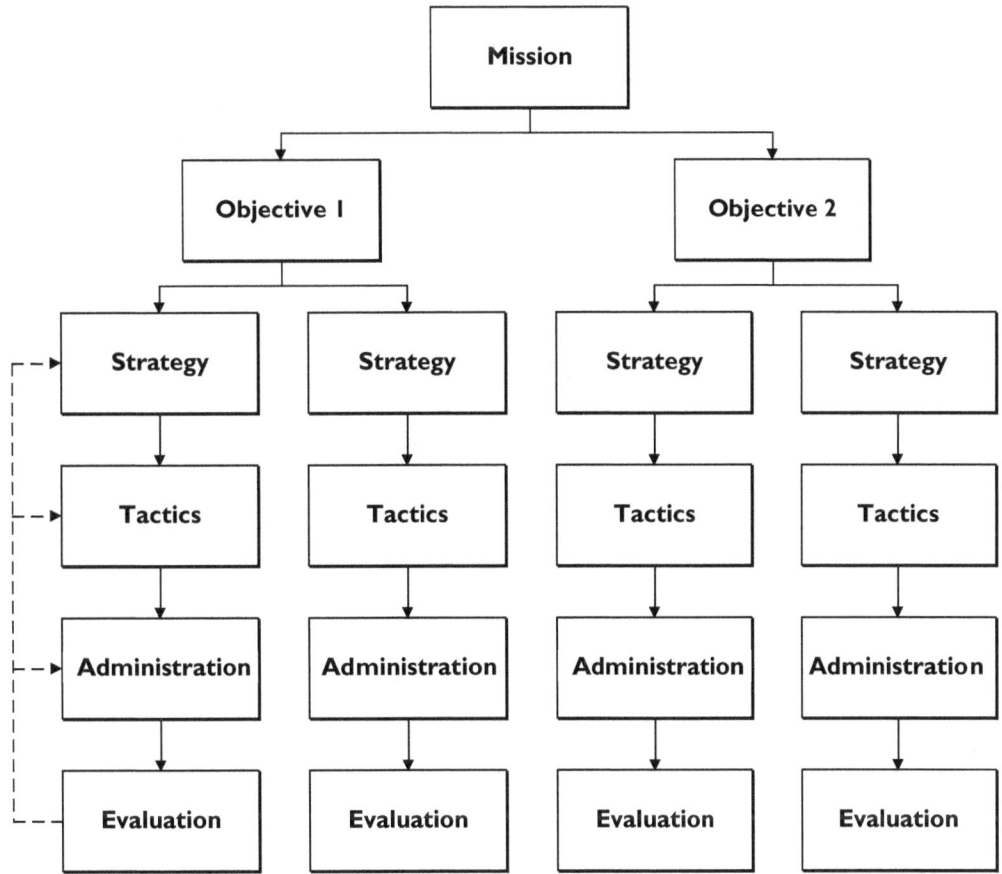

Although evaluation may be our last process, its importance should not be underestimated – evaluation helps us decide if our efforts have been effective, and sets the stage for maintaining or revising our strategy.

Again, we look at systematic procedures that will take us through all key aspects of newsletter publishing. And, consistent with our strategy throughout the book, we integrate evaluation with the other activities undertaken by managers.

In this section:
- *Profiling readers:* Segmentation techniques and application (Chapter 13)
- *Financial returns:* Simple ways of assessing if you're getting value for your money (Chapter 14)
- *Performance:* Assessing a newsletter's overall performance (Chapter 15)

Chapter 13
Profiling readers

In this chapter...

Throughout this book, we've used the term *targeted readers* almost as often as the word *readers* alone. That's because newsletters work best when they're sent to a carefully selected audience, not a mass audience.

The process of creating a targeted audience usually begins with some form of segmentation. And the most common form of segmentation is demographic – involving criteria like age, income, and education. Another, less common, form of segmentation is pyschographic, which involves criteria such as values, lifestyles, and social class.

In the first section of the chapter, we outline a number of segmentation criteria for both demographics and psychographics. We also look briefly at segmentation based on purchasing patterns, employment (employee newsletters), activity level (membership newsletters), industry classification, and size of organization.

In the second section, we explain how to profile readers, using segmentation information. Profiling readers helps us understand the *who* and the *what* of readership. Consider this knowledge an antidote to our natural inclination to project our own personalities onto our readers.

Select your readers

Back in Chapter 1 we noted that one reason for publishing a newsletter would be the existence of a niche audience, a relatively small segment of the population in general. That holds true in practice as well as theory, because effective newsletters don't try to attract a mass readership as newspapers and magazines do.

For employee and membership newsletters, selection of the audience is a straightforward process. The newsletter goes to all employees or to all members. It may also go to important stakeholders, but as soon as we include stakeholders, we've obviously selected another niche audience.

This targeting isn't so natural for marketing newsletters, and one of the key challenges for marketers is to define an audience that is neither too big nor too small. That, in turn, suggests prioritizing according to some criteria. And once we think about prioritizing, we're moving into the realm of segmentation, or classification, of readers. The two most common forms of segmentation are demographic and psychographic, but there are other, less common varieties as well.

Our skill in selecting criteria for segmentation may be as important as the content of the newsletter. Remember, we want to influence attitudes or behaviors, and having that goal is only reasonable on the assumption that members of the target group share an existing set of characteristics.

Know your readers

The more we know about those characteristics, the more likely it is that we'll be able to influence them. So, our thinking about segmentation shouldn't stop as soon we've created a list, or in the case of a membership or employee newsletter, after the list is created for us. The next step is to identify and understand the implications of their key characteristics; in other words, profile our readers.

We can create reader profiles using any of the criteria available to us. "How well educated are they?" might be a key question for the publisher of an employee newsletter. For a marketing newsletter, we might ask, "What is their annual income?" The more answers we have for questions like these, the more effective our newsletter will be.

While a full market research study might be best for finding the answers, there are considerations of cost and time. This chapter offers an alternative: a quick and inexpensive approach to building a profile of targeted readers. While it will not be as effective as proper research, it will certainly beat projecting our own needs and wants on our audience – something that happens far too frequently with newsletters.

Segmentation

Segmentation refers to the classification of readers as members of separate groups (segments), based on one or more characteristics. Each person is individual and unique, of course, but each shares one or more important characteristics with others. By grouping individuals with similar needs and interests, we can produce workable segments.

The most common form of segmentation is demographic, with psychographic a strong second. While the term psychographic may be unfamiliar to you, this method of segmentation is one that all of us use, informally and frequently. In addition to these two types, we briefly introduce several other types later in this chapter.

Segmentation can, and should, be applied to readers of any kind of newsletter, whether marketing, employee, membership, or other. The method may vary, the emphasis may shift, and the interpretation may change, but in the end, segmentation will help us understand and serve our readers.

Demographics

Demography is the science of vital and social statistics. Demographic analysis deals with criteria such as age, gender, marital status (married or single), income, education, and geographic location. All of these criteria, you'll notice, are easily measurable, and the segments mutually exclusive (for example, a reader's geographic location is either in some specific place, or it is not).

Age:

Age data is grouped into a relatively small number of ranges, rather than going year by year. For example, you might use these categories:
- Pre-teens
- Teens
- 18 - 24
- 25 - 34
- 35 - 44
- 45 - 54
- 55 - 64
- 65 +

If your readers are concentrated in just one or two of these segments, then it might be worthwhile to further subdivide them. An organization serving seniors, for example, could have a half-dozen segments above the age of 55, rather than just the two that come out of the scale above.

Income

Getting income information about or from individual persons can be tough, so you'll want to decide in advance how critical this information is to your profile. In many cases, you can use proxy information, such as occupation or the location of a reader's home, to get reasonably accurate indications of income. For example, if your readers are predominantly professional, then their incomes will likely reflect that fact.

One important secondary source we might use for incomes is census data. The various census reports provide income statistics at varying levels, from neighborhood to regional and national.

Consistency also can be a problem for income segmentation. Some sources show income by households, others by individual, or by estimates versus actual reports, or by averaging versus specific amounts. Each of these approaches has its advantages and disadvantages, but it's important that the same measures be used throughout your profiles.

Among income segmentation strategies, one of the two shown here will usually be appropriate:

- Low
- Medium
- High

Or

- $9,999 or less
- $10,000 to $19,999
- $20,000 to $29,999
- $30,000 to $39,999
- $40,000 to $49,999
- $50,000 to $99,999
- $100,000 or more

As you will have noted, the scale jumps to wider ranges at higher income levels, reflecting the expectation that fewer people will be in those ranges. Again, though, any individual segment can be expanded if it is of special interest.

Education

The most common segmentation uses the highest level of schooling completed, such as

- Elementary school
- High school
- College, technical school, or university.

Newsletter editors will be interested in education levels for two reasons: first, to know the level of education for specific informational objectives – to know how much explanation or background information is required, for example, and second, for reading capability. A newsletter must be understood to be effective, so the vocabulary and structure must be appropriate for readers' capabilities.

Location

This category of demographics usually refers to distance or accessibility. Increasing distances have several implications, including growing differences in language and culture. For example, some idiomatic expressions travel poorly between Great Britain and North America. Even at the local level, readers who live in an inner city neighborhood may understand words and concepts differently than readers who live in affluent suburbs.

One standard segmentation includes
- Neighborhood
- City
- Region
- Nation

Psychographics

Segmentation of populations according to values, lifestyles, or attitudes is called psychographic analysis. As you might expect from using criteria like these, psychographic distinctions are rarely as clear as demographic distinctions, and classifying individual readers by segments requires more subjective judgments.

Common psychographic segmentations include
- Values
- Lifestyles
- Social class

One well known psychographic segmentation is VALS, which stands for Values and Lifestyles. It divides consumers into four basic groups:
- Need-driven: those who purchase to satisfy subsistence needs
- Outer-directed: those who buy to impress others
- Inner-directed: those who want self-awareness

- Combined outer-and inner-directed: those who try to combine social and self orientations

Each of these groups can be subdivided further, if a larger number of categories is useful.

Another commonly used segmentation classifies adult lifestyles, which are easily observed and well understood, through direct or vicarious experience:
- Young singles
- Newly married
- Full nest (married, with children in the home)
- Empty nest (married, with no children living at home)
- Retired
- Solitary survivor (living alone after loss of spouse)

Regardless of the psychographic segmentation used, the objective remains the same: to understand readers by identifying the personal and social circumstances that affect and direct their lives. The type of segmentation that will be best depends on the needs of your organization and the objectives of its newsletter.

Other Segmentation Strategies

Our segmentation strategy need not be restricted to demographics and psychographics. Just about any characteristic can serve as a basis for segmenting a population, whether it's a population of people or of organizations. Listed below are a few commonly used segmentation strategies for readers of marketing, employee, and membership newsletters.

Purchasing Patterns:

Publishers of marketing newsletters can improve their odds of success by segmenting customers into categories such as
- Frequency of purchases
- Volume of purchases
- Service requirements
- Margin contribution

Employment criteria:

Readers of employee newsletters may be segmented in several ways:
- By function or department (such as operations, or sales)
- By hierarchical position, such as management or staff
- By years of service
- By eligibility or non-eligibility for benefits

Activity Level:
Membership organizations might segment according to these categories:
- Participation in organizational activities
- Attendance at meetings
- Service on committees, or as an officer

Industry Classification:
The most common segmentation by industry is the Standard Industrial Classification, referred to as SIC. It categorizes broad industry groupings, such as agriculture or retail trade, by two numbers. Additional digits narrow the segments within individual categories and the more numbers, the more specialized the classification.

Size of organization:
If you profile businesses or people who manage businesses, it may be prudent to segment by the size of firm. There are several options:
- Annual sales
- Number of employees
- Value of assets
- Capitalization

Multiple segmentation
The full range of readers can be segmented many times. For example, a political organization trying to attract new members might use demographic analysis to target 18- to 24-year-old females.

It would first divide the voting population as a whole into female and male segments, then segment the female group by ages. In addition, since political affiliations and sympathies reflect personal values, the party might plan to segment a third time, using psychographic criteria.

Segmentation always involves a trade-off between similarity and size. Each segmentation makes the target group smaller, but at the same time increases the degree of similarity among members of the group. Segmenting by gender, for example, cuts any given population roughly in half, but allows the publisher to focus on issues that concern either women or men.

Applying the process
The process involved in segmenting a reader population goes something like this:

- Define your targeted readers by specifying what they have in common, or how they (as a group) differ from the population as a whole.
- Identify which criteria are appropriate for segmenting them. Not all types listed above will fit your circumstances. Each manager must pick and choose, trying to find the few that provide the most useful information about readers. Again, remember the trade-off between similarity and size.
- Randomly select names from a list of targeted readers.
- Collect information about each criterion, for each selected name, through observation, surveys, or questionnaires.
- Group the results by the segmenting characteristics.
- Do other analysis, as necessary. For example, you might use cross-tabulation analysis, which involves looking at the relationships among criteria, and not at each criterion separately.
- Relate the results to the strategic questions asked in earlier chapters:
  > "What do we want readers to do as a result of reading our newsletter?"
  > "What do readers want?" (or "What do we have to give them to get them to read our newsletter?")

A quick profiling technique

If you have a limited amount of time, or a limited budget, or both, but you'd still like to do some analysis, consider this simple exercise.

1. At an editorial board meeting, with representatives of all stakeholders present, write the names of a number of readers or potential readers on cards, or list them on a piece of paper. Make sure you have at least 20, and more if possible. As many as 100 will work. These readers should be known to at least one member of the board, and preferably more than one.
2. From the group of names, randomly select at least 10 (and it is important that you make the selection random, doing something like blindly drawing cards or slips of paper from a hat).
3. Go through the names one at a time, and assess them according to the segmentation criteria you have chosen (note that these will be estimates in some cases). If possible, prepare the data in a table format.

The following table illustrates what the results might look like after you've gone through this exercise. Note that only a few of the many characteristics available to us have been used.

	Age	Income ($000s)	Education	Lifestyle*
Person 1	25 – 34	20 – 30	High School	YS
Person 2	35 – 44	50 – 100	University	FN
Person 3	25 – 34	30 – 40	Technical	NM
Person 4	25 – 34	30 – 40	College	YS
Person 5	18 – 24	20 – 30	Technical	YS
Person 6	25 – 34	30 – 40	College	FN
Person 7	35 – 44	40 – 50	High School	FN
Person 8	45 – 54	50 – 100	College	EN
Person 9	25 – 34	20 – 30	Technical	NM
Person 10	18 – 24	20 – 30	High School	YS

* YS = Young Single; NM = Newly Married; FN = Full Nest; EN = Empty Nest

Analyzing the results

In the age segment of our hypothetical audience, the following information can be noted or charted:

- 18 to 24 years = 2 persons
- 25 to 34 years = 5 persons
- 35 to 44 years = 2 persons
- 45 to 54 years = 1 person

For the income segment, the following information can be taken from the table:

- $20,000 to $29,999 = 4 persons
- $30,000 to $39,999 = 3 persons
- $40,000 to $49,999 = 1 person
- $50,000 to $100,000 = 2 persons

The following results emerge from the education segmentation:

- High school completed = 3 persons
- Technical school completed = 3 persons
- College completed = 3 persons
- University completed = 1 person

And looking at the lifestyles of the readers we're profiling, we see the following breakdown:

- Young Single = 4 persons
- Newly Married = 2 persons
- Full Nest = 3 persons
- Empty Nest = 1 person

From this brief exercise in segmentation we can make several observations:
- Half of all readers (5 out of 10) are between the ages of 25 and 34, and if that segment is extended by a unit of 1 in each direction (adding the 18–24 and 35–44 years), 9 of the 10 readers are represented.
- Incomes range between $20,000 and $40,000 for 7 out of 10, while the other 3 have incomes of more than $40,000.
- Education levels are fairly evenly mixed among 4 segments.
- The lifestyles reflect a young audience; 6 of the 10 are single or newly married with no children.

How confident can we be that this profile accurately reflects the profile of our entire reading audience? The answer depends on several factors:
- How randomly did we select readers for profiling? The greater the randomness, the more confidence we can have. In the ad hoc exercise above, we were limited by the need to assess characteristics from personal knowledge.
- How large was our sample? The sample we used was very small; some would say not nearly large enough. And up to certain limits, the larger the size, the greater the confidence. (Consult reference sources about the size of sample needed for audience size.)
- How well did we design the profile and the exercise? Obviously, much depends on which characteristics we selected and which ones we left out. Keep in mind that survey design is both an art and a demanding science.
- How accurate were our assessments? How thorough is our knowledge of the people we profiled? Could personal feelings have affected our judgement?

All in all, our little exercise has several weak spots, and can hardly be expected to produce results as reliable as those from professional market research or surveys. Still, we have a set of results that can tell us a good deal. And what we have is much better than simply projecting our own personalities and views onto readers.

To increase our confidence in the results of this profiling, we could do several things. One would be to work with the names of more readers (assuming we know something about each). Another would involve asking readers themselves to do the assessment. And, of course, studying questionnaire design and data interpretation would increase our skill in developing and administering such exercises.

A few more words about psychographic profiling

At first glance, assessing the psychographic characteristics of persons you barely know may seem an intimidating task, but there are many clues that will help. For example, what subjects do they raise in conversation or seem eager to discuss? How do they dress? How do they make choices about the products they buy? What sorts of photos or documents do they put on their office walls? These clues may not lead to accurate assessments every time, but they will provide a rough guide for quick profiling.

As we noted earlier, psychographic segmentation involves subjective judgments, unless you're doing very sophisticated research. But subjective judgment can be informative, as long you can apply it consistently across all the people you're evaluating.

The *whom* and the *what*

As the preceding exercise suggests, profiling readers by segmentation analysis helps us understand the *whom* and the *what* of readership. It provides valuable information that ensures we know our readers better than when we started. In addition, it challenges our assumptions about readers, and the natural inclination to generalize, simplify, or project our own personalities onto them.

Another important benefit of segmentation and profiling is that it forces us to focus outwardly. Newsletters can fail because of an inward focus; that is, they can deal with what the publisher wants the readers to do, and overlook what the readers want from the publisher. Such newsletters end up becoming a form of brochure, but being neither true newsletter nor real brochure, they do the jobs of both poorly.

Chapter 14
Costs and returns

In this chapter...

"Is it worthwhile to add more names to our mailing list?"
(See the section on *Fixed and Variable Costs*)

"Are there any economies of scale if we increase the size of our mailing list?"
(See *Fixed and Variable Costs*)

"How will the cost of a newsletter affect our profits?"
(See *Break-even Analysis*)

"Will the newsletter be cost-effective for increasing employee productivity?"
(See *Cost per Employee and Hours per Employee*)

"Can our non-profit organization afford a newsletter?"
(See *Cost per Member*)

In this chapter, we introduce a number of ideas for assessing the financial costs and returns of newsletters, whether marketing, employee, or membership. Using simple arithmetic, formulas, and concepts, we report on or develop a number of tools that managers can use quickly and easily.

A return on your newsletter investment

A newsletter is a tool to advance the interests of the organization that publishes it. If that advancement has financial overtones, whether direct or indirect, then we need to know whether the newsletter provides an adequate return for the resources invested in it.

In the case of a marketing newsletter, for example, we want to know whether it generates enough new business or retains enough existing business to cover its costs and provide a return. Or, administrators of associations may be concerned about the cost of recruiting members with a newsletter.

All this leads us to ask how we can measure returns generated by newsletters. How can we be sure the newsletter is a cost-effective tool for advancing our objectives, if we don't have workable measures?

In this chapter, we introduce a few measures that address the issue of costs and returns. For marketing newsletters, we'll borrow some concepts from management accounting. For employee and membership newsletters, we've created measures of our own.

We can't guarantee that these measures will give you definitive answers or that they will fully assess your newsletter. But the process may be just as important as the results: by working through the measures, you will gain a much better understanding of the components of cost and return, and of the relationships among them.

One other note: no special financial or mathematical skills are required to use these tools. We've kept them simple and straightforward, so anyone can use them without undue strain. On the other hand, if you enjoy working with numbers, you may wish to go beyond this chapter. In that case, a good starting point would be a textbook on management accounting.

Costs

Usually we know our budgetary costs: so much for getting articles and photos, a particular fee for desktop publishing or layout, and our printing and distribution costs. In addition, we have at least a rough idea of how many hours go into each issue.

So, most of the information we need for our analyses will be available from the budget figures developed in Chapter 10, where we introduced newsletter budgets. To that, we'll add Table 14–1, which segments the analyses in this chapter by type of newsletter: marketing, employee, and membership.

	Marketing Newsletter	Employee Newsletter	Membership Newsletter
Fixed & Variable Costs	✓	✓	✓
Break-even	✓		✓
Cost per Employee		✓	
Hours per Employee		✓	
Cost per Member	✓		✓

✓ indicates that this analysis applies to this type of newsletter.

Fixed and Variable Costs

"What are the costs of adding more names to our mailing list?"

If you're putting together a mailing list for a marketing newsletter, you usually have some choices about the number of names on it. Unlike employee and membership newsletters, a marketing newsletter usually does not have a narrowly-defined audience – the size of the list can be increased or reduced according to the objectives. To identify how costs will change according to the size of the list, you can use fixed and variable costs analysis.

Fixed costs remain the same, regardless of the number of copies or the size of the mailing. For example, the costs of staffing and laying out the newsletter don't change, no matter how many copies are printed.

Variable costs, on the other hand, do vary with the number of copies printed. There are two common variable expenses for newsletters. One is printing, with printers billing according to the number of copies produced. The other common variable expense is distribution, assuming the newsletter is mailed or you pay to have it delivered to individual readers.

If you publish an electronic or online newsletter, you may not have any variable costs at all. Of course, you may incur a variable expense if your Internet Service Provider charges you according to the volume of data moved, and you e-mail a very high quantity.

For established, printed newsletters, the easiest way to determine fixed and variable expenses is with basic addition and subtraction:

Variable costs = printing + distribution
Fixed cost = full cost – variable costs

For example:
Printing $800
Mailing $500
Total variable costs $1,300

and

    Full cost per issue . . . .$3,000   (You calculated this in Ch. 10)
    Less variable costs . . . .<u>$1,300</u>
    Fixed cost per issue $1,700

Economies of scale

Now, let's use this knowledge of fixed and variable costs to figure out how costs will change if we increase the size of a mailing list, say from 1,000 copies to 5,000 copies.

We'll start by considering the nature of printing and mailing costs. Printing costs include a setup charge, plus a small amount for each copy. Setup charges cover the printer's costs for pre-press services, administration, and a portion of overhead. Per-copy costs cover press time, paper, and ink.

The price you pay – the combined cost – includes both the setup charge and the charge per copy, which you'll now recognize as the printer's fixed and variable costs. Obviously, the greater the number of copies, the lower the fixed cost allocated to each copy will be. That's why the cost per copy decreases as the number of printed copies increases: it's an economy of scale.

For example, let's say a printer charges $800 for one thousand copies. Of that sum, $500 goes to setup expenses and other one-time costs, and then 30 cents per copy for the number of copies printed (1,000 copies x 30 cents = $300.00). If the shop prints 5,000 copies, it still charges $500 for setup and 30 cents per copy, but now the $500 setup fee is spread over 5,000 copies (at 10 cents each), rather than, say, 1,000 copies (at 50 cents each).

Let's look at the way your costs change each time you add a thousand copies, using the prices above:

Number of Copies	Total Cost	Cost per Copy
1,000	$800	$0.80
2,000	$1,100	$0.55
3,000	$1,400	$0.47
4,000	$1,700	$0.43
5,000	$2,000	$0.40

Turning to mailing, the regular cost of mail will be the number of pieces (copies) multiplied by the cost per piece. Or, if you reach certain threshold volumes, you may qualify for bulk mail rates. That, too, involves the equivalent of a setup fee, plus a fee per piece.

To return to the question with which we began this section, the answer is *Yes:* the overall cost will go up, but the cost per copy will go down as volume increases. And because the increase won't be linear, it may be worthwhile to increase the size of the list.

Whether or not an increase will be worthwhile depends on reader responses. That, in turn, takes us back to the issues discussed in the *Strategy* and *Tactics* sections.

Break-even analysis
"How will the cost of a newsletter affect our profits?"

Break-even analysis tells us how many units of product must be sold at a given price, to cover both the fixed and variable costs – in other words, to break even on costs and revenues. For marketing newsletters, it will be the number of units that must be sold to exactly offset the costs involved in producing and selling them (before profits). In the case of a membership organization, it may be the number of memberships that must be sold to cover the cost of recruiting and member services. You'll find this measure helpful in identifying how much you must achieve with a newsletter before you start getting back more than you put into it.

The factors that go into the break-even equation are revenue, fixed costs, variable costs, and profit. Here's how they might be described for the company as a whole:
- Revenue = number of units sold, multiplied by selling price per unit
- Fixed cost = overhead, and costs that do not change with volume
- Variable cost = varies directly with volume, for example, labor costs
- Profit = zero for true break-even, or a specific dollar figure to match current profits or a desired level of profit

Usually we want to know how many units we have to sell at a given price before we begin earning a profit. That question can be set up this way:

Revenue = fixed costs + variable costs + profit (of zero)

Revenue, you'll recall, equals number of units sold, multiplied by the price per unit.

Or, if we know how many units we expect to sell, but want to know how much to charge for each one, we can transpose the various elements in the equation. Similarly, we can solve the equation for any of the elements in it.

A break-even example
The XYZ Briefcase Company is considering a marketing newsletter. It wants to know how many additional briefcases it would need to sell to cover the

extra cost of producing and distributing the newsletter. The company's current situation is shown below, on an annualized (yearly) basis:

> Revenue (1,000 units @ $100) $100,000
> Less fixed costs (without a newsletter) . . . . ($45,000)
> Less variable costs (1,000 units @ $40.) . . . . . . ($40,000)
> Profit $15,000

In words, this tells us the company now earns a profit of $15,000 on sales of $100,000, based on fixed costs of $45,000 and variable costs of $40,000.

Let's say a newsletter will increase these fixed costs by $10,000 a year – the total cost of the newsletter – for a new total fixed cost of $55,000. It is also expected to increase sales, so *total* variable costs will rise by $40 per unit, although the variable cost *per unit* remains the same.

Because total variable costs are rising, we can't simply divide the additional cost of the newsletter ($10,000.00) by the amount of revenue brought in by each sale of a briefcase ($100.00). So, how do we figure out how many more brief cases must be sold? That's where we use the break-even equation.

It shows us how many extra briefcases must be sold to cover the cost of the newsletter, and still maintain the current profit of $15,000. We use the letter 'y' as the symbol for the number of units:

> Revenue = fixed costs + variable costs + profit, or
> $100(y units) = $55,000 + $40(y units) + $15,000 or,
> 100y = $55,000 + 40y + $15,000

Solving the equation:

> $100y − $40y = $55,000 + $15,000
> $60y = $70,000
> y = 1,166 units (briefcases)

From this, we can see the company must sell an additional 166 briefcases (the current 1,000 + 166) to cover the $10,000 cost of its proposed newsletter and still maintain profits at the current level. If it sells fewer than 166 additional briefcases, profit will decrease to less than $15,000; if it sells more than 166, the profit will increase to more than $15,000.

We should note that this example is necessarily simplified, and that the findings of break-even analysis only work within specified ranges for fixed and variable expense values. Also, for companies with many products, break-even analysis will be more complex, as fixed costs are allocated among them.

Managers and editors of marketing newsletters, though, will find it useful to know in principle how newsletter costs and returns affect a company's bottom line. And a general idea of how many additional units must be sold to cover the costs of their newsletters should be helpful.

Measures for employee newsletters

"Will a newsletter be cost effective for increasing employee productivity?"

Cost per employee per issue

Our basic measure for employee newsletters is *cost per employee per issue*. The calculation is straightforward: Divide the total cost of an issue of the newsletter by the number of employees. If, for example, the total cost per issue is $2,400 and it goes to 200 employees, the cost per employee per issue is $12.

With a figure like that in mind, it becomes possible to start asking whether we're getting a reasonable return. If the newsletter is published monthly, for example, we can ask whether the newsletter increases the productivity of each employee by $12 per month.

Returns will be greatest in organizations with the highest dependence on employee skills, expertise, or attitudes. In the normal course of events, they may spend thousands of dollars each month in training or continuing education. In such cases, it's not hard to see how spending $12 per month per employee on a newsletter might be a good investment.

That's also true for a service company that offers a high level of customer service, and depends on the skills of its employees. On the other hand, a company with a large, unskilled workforce might find that too expensive. Whatever the case, the key is to assess the cost in terms of the objectives.

In some cases, the newsletter manager may get a better sense of a newsletter's potential or current effectiveness by taking this measure a step further, to *hours per employee per issue*.

Hours per employee per issue

To calculate *hours per employee per issue*
1. Divide the total wages and benefit costs for the newsletter period (we use monthly as an example) by the number of employees,
2. Divide again, by the number of hours worked in an average month (for example, 176 hours, a figure reached by multiplying 22 working days by 8 hours). The result is the average hourly cost per employee.
3. Divide the cost per employee per issue (calculated in the preceding section) by the average hourly cost per employee.

Let's work out the numbers for a hypothetical company:
1. The basic figures:
    - Average monthly wage and benefits cost to the company is $600,000
    - There are 200 employees
    - The average cost per employee, per month, is $3,000
2. The average hourly cost per employee:
    - $600,000 ÷ 200 employees ÷ 176 hours = $17.
3. The hours per employee per issue:
    - Assume that the newsletter costs $2,400 per issue
    - The cost per issue per employee will be $2,400 divided by 200 employees = $12.00
    - $12 divided by $17 = .71 hours or 42 minutes per month

In this example, we see the newsletter costs the equivalent of 42 minutes of employee time per month (not including reading time). Knowing that, we can decide whether the newsletter will deliver value for the money.

Will it reduce the amount of work time that employees would otherwise spend asking Human Resources staff about benefits? Will it increase productivity per employee by 42 minutes a month by showing employees more efficient ways to handle customer inquiries?

From another perspective, we know that adding another employee would add an average 176 hours a month to the payroll. But we also could gain 176 hours per month, without adding staff, by increasing productivity. For a company with 200 employees, it would mean increasing productivity by .88 hours (53 minutes) per employee, either all at once, or in stages.

That leads us the question, "How much will the newsletter improve productivity?" And that, in turn, takes us back to one of the fundamental questions we asked at the beginning of the book: "What do we want readers to do as a result of reading our newsletter?" We've now reached a point where this question is both meaningful and answerable, and should lead us to an effective employee newsletter.

Measures for member newsletters

"Can our non-profit association afford a newsletter?"

Cost per member per year

Here, we use a measurement similar to the cost per employee per issue. This measurement is *cost per member per year*. It assumes that dues will be charged and collected on an annual basis. Therefore, we use the annual cost of publishing the newsletter as a base.

For example,
- An organization with 1,000 members is considering a membership-relations newsletter that would cost $10,000 per year (for both fixed and variable expenses)
- The cost per member per year, therefore, will be $10

With this figure, and other information such as average annual dues and cost of membership services, the organization can decide whether a newsletter is affordable, and assess whether or not it might be cost effective. By quantifying in this way, it's possible to make many decisions about whether or not a newsletter should be started or continued.

We also can use fixed and variable costs to set the membership newsletter strategy. Fixed costs, you'll recall, remain the same, regardless of the number of copies printed and distributed. Variable costs, like those for printing and mailing, go up and down according to the number of copies.

Let's consider the plan for a hypothetical membership newsletter for an organization with 1,000 members, and a newsletter budget of $10,000. Using conventional publishing and distribution techniques, we'll print and mail 1,000 copies, four times each year. Assuming the cost of printing and mailing is $1 per copy per occasion, then we need $4,000 of the total budget for that purpose. That leaves $6,000 a year for fixed expenses, or $1,500 per issue, for services such as freelance writing, editing, and page layout.

Or, we might ask about increasing our mailing list: What would happen if we sent the newsletter to prospective members as well as paid-up members? By segmenting the fixed and variable costs, we could explain to the Board of Directors that doubling the mailing list to 2,000 names would increase the cost per issue by $1,000 and the annual cost by $4,000. That gives the Board a solid number against which to estimate the number of new members who might join, and how much the additional dues income might be.

Let's now use this information to draw some conclusions about newsletters and membership organizations. In doing so, we'll look at four combinations of dues and members (all are relative values, of course).

Many members, low dues:
An organization with many members and low dues (such as a political party, for example) should be very sensitive about the costs of its newsletter, and particularly about variable costs (printing and distribution). Because variable costs will be relatively high, it may not be worthwhile to use a printed

newsletter as a recruiting tool. However, electronic (Internet or other) or fax distribution might be a good idea since there are no significant variable costs.

Few members, high dues:
If there are relatively few members and high dues, the organization should be concerned about fixed costs. The loss of even a few members might strain it's finances. On the other hand, if the newsletter brings in only a few new members, the return will be relatively high. Any newsletter, whether electronic or printed, will be risky.

Many members, high dues:
If an organization can attract many members even though the dues are high, then it's obviously doing something very well. In this situation, a newsletter would seem highly useful, both to keep existing members and to attract new ones. There shouldn't be any significant concern about either fixed or variable costs, and a newsletter could be launched with little risk.

Few members, low dues:
In the opposite corner is an organization with relatively few members and low dues. It has to be concerned about fixed costs, because they must be divided among a limited number of members. And variable costs also may be a factor, if there aren't enough copies printed or distributed to reach threshold volumes. Given the concern about fixed costs, even electronic or fax distribution may not be worth considering.

The Multi-purpose Newsletter

For the sake of simplicity, we've assumed the analytical tools described in this chapter will be applied to single-purpose newsletters. Yet, in real life, newsletters rarely have just one objective. A newsletter may be both an employee newsletter and a marketing newsletter, for instance. Or an association might use its newsletter as a marketing tool, to bring in new members, and a retention tool, to keep existing members.

Allocations are rarely simple and straightforward. Most often, one objective blends into another, or priorities shift from issue to issue. To make allocations in these circumstances, we'll need to go back to the strategy questions: What do we want readers to do? What do readers want from us?

Reviewing the objectives may bring our purposes back into focus. But we must accept the fact that most divisions will be more or less artificial, and will require that we make some subjective judgments.

Chapter 15
Assessing performance

In this chapter...

To complete our discussion of newsletter management, we take a look at the kind of evaluation that might be done periodically by a manager or members of an editorial board. This chapter also concludes the book, as it recaps all the critical points made about strategic communication with a newsletter.

Again, our evaluation is strategically oriented, which means that it focuses on the objectives the newsletter is designed to help the organization achieve. Our assessment starts with a comparison between what we set out to do – the objectives – and what's been accomplished.

If the goal has been met, we can proclaim the newsletter a success and go on to set new objectives. But if not, then we need to go through the process outlined in this chapter.

Strategic issues include considerations of how appropriate the medium is for the objectives, how well we have articulated what it is we want readers to do, and how well we knew or know what readers want.

In the realm of tactics, we review whether or not the content was relevant and credible, the presentation was appropriate for the readers, the frequency of publication was sufficient, and the number of pages was appropriate.

Finally, we review management of the newsletter, whether by an editorial board or individual manager, and look briefly at responsibility for implementing changes based on the evaluation.

Getting Started

A key responsibility for those who manage a newsletter is periodic assessment or evaluation. The newsletter uses resources – at least money and time, and perhaps other resources – and we should know whether we're getting a return on that investment.

If targeted readers did what we wanted them to do, and did it in great enough numbers, then we've been successful. For instance, if enough readers bought something from us because they read our marketing newsletter, then the newsletter should be considered a success. Or, if enough employees decided to learn to use computers because of their employee newsletter, then it helped achieve an objective.

If we moved closer to our objective(s) as planned, or achieved it (them), then our assessment can end here. Quite simply, the newsletter worked, and we can get on with setting new objectives or a new function for the newsletter. On the other hand, if it didn't help us reach our objectives, then we need to go through the evaluation process that follows. However, before the evaluation begins, we should decide on the measures to use, and on responsibility for changes.

Measures

How do we measure the objectives and accomplishments? Do we have some non-subjective criteria? Do we have quantifiable benchmarks that tell us where to start? Our assessment can be intuitive, of course, but that reduces the confidence we can place in it. Measures are a critical issue, one that must be resolved before we proceed with the assessment.

Appropriate measures might include the number of leads generated by a marketing newsletter, the productivity of staff for an employee newsletter, and member participation for a membership newsletter.

In some cases, it may be necessary to create tools for measuring. For example, if we want to know about the effect of a newsletter on some aspect of employee productivity, we may need to survey workers at the beginning and end of some set period. The results at the beginning of the period would be a benchmark against which to assess the results at the end of the period.

With measures determined, we can return to some of the analytical tools in Chapter 14, *Costs and Returns*. That chapter, however, deals only with financial issues, while the thrust of this chapter is to consider all aspects of progress toward our objectives.

Responsibilities

You also need to know who is responsible for the changes that may be required. Assuming changes are needed, some obviously rest with management, some with staff. If a change is one that management must make, does it go to the editorial board, or do the evaluators make the changes? If the changes involve staff, what process will be used and what ratification provided? These will be simple problems if addressed in advance, before the evaluation begins, or when the terms of reference for evaluation are set. They may not be so easy later, after changes begin.

It may be prudent, as well, to determine the *what* and *how* of reporting to others. If you plan to make significant changes to the newsletter, it may be wise to let readers know in advance. Similarly, senior management should know of changes in advance, and of the implications of those changes.

Did readers do what we wanted them to do?

The right medium?

Should we have used a newsletter, or would another medium have been more effective? Another medium can be anything from face-to-face discussion to television advertising. And in the first phase of the assessment, we really only need to ask whether we chose the right one.

Having the ability to produce a newsletter is not a reason to have one. Instead, a newsletter should be used when one or more of these key demand criteria are present:
- Expectations among stakeholders
- Niche audiences
- Complex issues, and a need for specialized communication vehicles
- Internal development of staff communication skills
- Control over subject matter, timing, cost, and context

If none of these apply, then perhaps emphasis should be shifted from the newsletter to another medium. This might involve shutting down the newsletter altogether, or at least diverting some of the resources dedicated to it. Of course, you may have specific circumstances that make a newsletter mandatory.

An alternative approach, if none of the reasons above apply, may be the one delineated in Chapter 11. There, we explain how the reach of a newsletter can be extended by using it as a media relations tool.

If, after considering all the information here and the information gleaned so far in your assessment, a newsletter seems to be an appropriate tool, then it's time to move on to the next question.

Appropriate objectives?

What did we want readers to do as a result of reading the newsletter? Has this objective for the newsletter been articulated and written down? Is it possible to quantify it, so we can actually measure whether or not we reached the objective or made progress toward it?

It may be helpful to go back to the matrix showing change vs. reinforcement, and behavior vs. attitude:

1. Reinforce an attitude
2. Change an attitude
3. Reinforce a behavior
4. Change a behavior.

In addition, we need to know whether the objective was achievable, given the resources available to us. And we must be sure to get that relationship in the right order: the resources should fit the objective; not the other way around. If we work on the premise that the newsletter should be tailored to the resources, and not the objective, then any assessment becomes meaningless.

In assessing objectives for the newsletter, also review events of the previous year (or other period), and look for external factors that might have had an effect. These could be anything from economic conditions in the national economy to simple delivery problems.

Did we serve reader needs?

The third strategy point to be assessed is our effectiveness at serving reader needs. Only by responding to readers' needs do we get them to read our newsletter, and thus expose themselves to our messages. And that raises the issue of what they want. What will help them achieve their goals and objectives, or help them make difficult choices?

If we can't say with certainty what they want, then we need some readership research: perhaps market research or reader surveys. Another option is the profiling exercise illustrated in Chapter 13. From that profile we should be able to articulate and prioritize the needs of readers.

This is also a good time to consider focus. After all, if we're trying to serve too many target audiences, or too many segments within one audience, we probably can't serve any one of them very well.

Did we provide the right content?

In the strategy section of the assessment process, we discussed the objectives or needs of the publisher, as well as the needs and wants of the reader, but we discussed them separately. When we get to content, though, we address them jointly.

As we found in Chapter 5, good subjects are those that serve both publisher and reader – at the same time. The publisher wants content that persuades readers to respond in the desired way. The reader wants subjects that help her realize her goals in life.

Subjects that serve both publisher and reader are said to be in the shared environment. And any assessment of content will mean reviewing the boundaries of the shared environment, to ensure the boundaries are appropriate, and that we stayed within them.

Reviewing the boundaries means checking for relevance and credibility. Relevance refers to the type of subject matter selected. Examples include the organization and industry for an employee newsletter, the product or service for a marketing newsletter, and the shared cause for a membership newsletter.

Credibility exists when readers perceive the newsletter's publishers to be well informed about the subjects they've selected. In your assessment, you should ask whether readers see the newsletter and the people behind it as possessing some special knowledge, experience, or qualifications.

And we want to know whether readers generally understood the content. It may not have been understood if the writing was too difficult, if the concepts were too advanced for the audience, or for a number of other reasons. We'll explore those reasons in the next section.

How was our presentation?

In assessing presentation, we go back to three key elements of willingness:
- How involved are the readers?
- What kind of emotion do they bring to the newsletter?
- How consistent are the newsletter messages with the values and beliefs held by the readers?

Our choice of voices depends on our assessment in each of these categories. The list of possible voices includes *challenge, analyze, entertain, consult, envision, empathize, advise or inform, teach, interpret,* and *solve.* Some feasible combinations are listed below:

- Low involvement: challenge or entertain the reader
- Moderate involvement: consult, envision, advise, solve
- High involvement: advise, teach, interpret, solve

- Negative emotion: challenge, analyze, empathize
- Neutral emotion: entertain, envision, interpret, solve
- Positive emotion: consult, advise, solve

- Low consistency: challenge, analyze, interpret, solve
- Moderate consistency: envision, solve
- High consistency: consult, advise, teach.

Allowing latitude for both our interpretation of the situation and mastery of the voices, we can go on to ask how well we matched involvement, emotion, and consistency with the voices available to us.

Should we have used different voices or more voices? Perhaps fewer voices? That's one of the issues that an assessment team will want to consider carefully as it evaluates its newsletter.

Often enough?

Was our frequency of publication commensurate with the willingness of readers to do what we wanted them to do? The more exposures in a specific time period, the greater the likelihood we'll get the response we want from readers. In addition to the simple issue of exposures per time period, there are also opportunities to repeat the message in different forms – one of the strengths of newsletters.

So, our assessment of newsletter effectiveness should include a review of willingness and frequency. If readers were relatively unwilling, did we publish frequently enough to get them to respond? If they were willing, did we publish too often, wasting resources?

We also argued that publishers of employee and marketing newsletters should assume at least some degree of unwillingness on the part of readers. That unwillingness is inherent in the relationship between employee and employer, and between seller and buyer, and does not necessarily reflect on managerial competence or the integrity of the publisher's organization. For a membership organization, though, we can assume generally willing readers in normal circumstances.

The right number of pages?

Were readers able to do what we asked of them? If not, then we probably needed more pages, so we could provide more information, better explanations, more repetition, or other space-consuming content. Again, we're referring to the ability of readers to do or think as we request, and not to their ability to read the newsletter. That was covered in an earlier section. For the person or team doing the evaluation, the best starting point is likely to be a delineation of the steps a reader must take to respond.

If you publish a marketing newsletter, for example, and you want customers to buy more or buy more often, then you'd do a review of the steps involved in making a purchase. They might be awareness, managing the cost (through installment payments, for example), traveling to the store, and getting the product home, to cite a few. Once we know the steps the reader must take to respond, then we can review the number of articles required, and the amount of space required for each.

Did we manage well?

Whether the newsletter is managed by one person or by an editorial board, and whether you do all of the publishing tasks or delegate them, the issue of management should be part of the evaluation process. We can ask a number of questions about our management structure, practices, and procedures.

Assuming a board manages the newsletter, does the board represent readers and stakeholders adequately? Is information from stakeholders getting to the board, and is the board passing that information on to the editor and staff?

Has the board set appropriate policies for the newsletter? Have the ideas and assumptions underpinning the newsletter been examined and articulated? The biggest issue in policy making is the linkage between strategy and operations – between what readers are supposed to do and what editorial activity is required.

The adequacy of supervision should be considered: the extent to which the board has maintained an ongoing vigilance. Have the editor or newsletter staff slipped into habits or practices that detract from the effectiveness of the newsletter? At the same time, has the board avoided interfering with the tasks of people who do the work? Journalism requires a body of knowledge and skills that members of the board probably don't have, so they should be cautious about getting too involved in that area.

Finally, did the newsletter get the resources and support it required, to function at the level of effectiveness demanded? That includes not only money and facilities, whether through budgets or otherwise, but also information, which is a critical resource for a communication vehicle.

New objectives

To conclude this process, we go back to our objectives. Now that we know what we gained or failed to gain, we're better equipped to deal with objectives. Those that were easily accomplished probably weren't demanding enough. Those that eluded us completely may not have been feasible at all.

Evaluation, remember, is a means to an end, and that end is the accomplishment or advancement of objectives. By methodically and regularly assessing our newsletter, we improve our ability to set appropriate objectives. And new objectives are the final step.

In conclusion

With this chapter, we have concluded our discussion of newsletter management. It included a review of the critical functions that managers and others responsible for newsletters must confront.

From a broader perspective, this book has argued that a newsletter should be a tool for strategic communication – communication driven by objectives. For your newsletter to work effectively, both your objectives and those of your readers should be addressed.

A newsletter, we must remember, represents a bargain between publisher and reader, with the reader receiving helpful information in exchange for viewing persuasive messages posted by the publisher. And bargains with benefits for both parties last longest and work best.

Good publishing!

Appendix I
Glossary

Benchmark: a starting measure or baseline with which subsequent measures can be compared. The process of establishing these measures and comparing subsequent results, for competitive advantage, is called *benchmarking*.

Demand factors: the changes in organizations, and society as a whole, that created demand for narrowly targeted communication vehicles like newsletters.

Desktop publishing: the use of computers and specialized software to prepare documents for the printing process. It mainly involves the arrangement of text, graphics, and design on a page.

Editor: a person in charge of non-advertising operations in any medium. The editor reports to the publisher, while journalists, artists, and others report to the editor.

Market research: a methodical investigation into the size or characteristics of a group of people. Techniques include focus groups, surveys, questionnaires, statistical analysis, and systematic observation.

Marketing: while the word *marketing* often is used interchangeably with selling, a more formal definition describes marketing as research and decisions about markets, products that satisfy those markets, the channels through which the markets are served, and the prices at which products are sold.

Media relations: the practice of developing relationships with journalists and editors, so they will provide coverage or more favorable coverage. The practice works best when both parties benefit from the arrangement.

Medium/media/mass media: a medium is a channel for communication, such as a newspaper. Media is the plural of medium, and mass media refers to the communication channels with very large audiences: traditionally radio, television, newspapers, and magazines.

Mission: an organization's defining goal or overarching aim, often expressed formally in a mission statement. For example, "The XYZ Corporation will be the nation's leading supplier of hospital laundry equipment." May also be called a vision statement.

Model: a simplified representation of reality, created to illustrate key relationships and sequences. Business models help us understand important processes, including human actions and business practices.

Newsletter: a document distributed to a specific audience; free newsletters advance the objectives of the publisher, while subscription newsletters provide information for which the receiver pays.

> *Non-subscription newsletter:* a bargain between publisher and reader in which the publisher provides useful information to readers at no charge, and readers open themselves to the publisher's attempts to influence the way they satisfy their needs.
>
> *Strategic newsletter:* one in which the information provided aligns with the objectives of the publishing organization and the needs of targeted readers, with the aim of helping the publishing organization achieve its objectives.

Niche: a specific sector of a population, made up of people who share one or more important characteristics. The term niche audience often is used interchangeably with targeted audience, although targeted suggests a more active approach to defining the sector.

Objective: a specific goal or target that provides a measure of success or failure. For example, "The sales department will sign up 500 new customers by June 30th." While not all objectives contain specific quantities or times, those that do are more likely to produce the desired results.

Persuasion: influencing the way people act or think, by making an appeal to their rationality or emotions. It requires voluntary compliance — and does not include coercion or manipulation.

Process: the steps involved in doing a job or project. For example, a plant might have a parts manufacturing process, an assembly process, and a shipping process. Each process may be made up of a number of sub-processes.

Profiling readers: an exercise in which readers are divided into groups, according to pre-set categories and characteristics. Most commonly associated with customer or marketing newsletters.

Proofs: the documents that are checked before printing begins, to look for errors and omissions. For example, blueline proofs that printing companies supply to customers for final checks of text and graphics.

Publisher: in the mass media, it is the person in charge of all operations, including advertising and editorial content; the equivalent of a president or chief executive officer. For an organizational newsletter, the publisher may be the organization, the manager responsible for it, or both.

Quality movement: a highly rational (analytical and knowledge-based) approach to management. Total Quality Management (TQM) involves the systematic improvement of processes, while Quality Assurance (QA) refers to preventive measures such as standardized procedures and inspections.

Segmentation: dividing populations into groups with shared characteristics (see also *Niche*). Two common forms are demographic and psychographic, which refer to groupings based on vital statistics and lifestyles/attitudes respectively.

Shared Environment: The range of subjects in which publisher and readers have a common interest. These subjects will be relevant to both, and readers will be able to judge the publisher's credibility.

Stakeholder: literally, someone who holds a stake in the fortunes of an organization; less formally, a member of a group on which an organization depends, such as a customer, employee, investor, supplier, or member (often a reciprocal dependence).

Strategy: a relatively abstract plan for achieving an objective; it sets out a direction or approach to the objective, rather than specific plans (covered under *Tactics*). For example, "Our strategy for increasing market share is to provide the best customer service."

Supply factors: the technology and knowledge that made possible the profusion of newsletters among both for-profit and not-for-profit organizations.

Tactics: specific plans for realizing a strategy. While strategy covers the general direction, tactics deals with how something will be accomplished. For example, "To deliver the best customer service, we will respond to all inquiries within two hours, …"

Tasks: the actual actions taken to implement a tactic. For example, "To ensure all inquiries are addressed within two hours, technical support will monitor incoming e-mail, and customer service will handle telephone calls."

Appendix II
Further reading

It may be one of the truisms of learning and reading that every question answered prompts more questions. After reading this book, you will have a solid understanding of newsletter foundations. At the same time, though, you will undoubtedly have new questions about newsletters, management, and communication.

With that in mind, I've prepared the following list for further reading. It includes books, articles, and Web sites that you may find helpful in pursuing your new questions. It provides starting points, of course, rather than a comprehensive list. Beyond this list, talk to booksellers and librarians about your needs. Their help will make your search both faster and more productive.

Newsletters

The following resources complement *A Manager's Guide to Newsletters: Communicating for Results*. They provide information about non-managerial aspects of newsletter publishing, including journalism and design.

> Beach, Mark, *Editing your newsletter: how to produce an effective publication using traditional tools and computers*, 4th edition. Cincinnati, Writer's Digest Books, 1995. A classic treatment of writing, design, and other production issues.
>
> Beach, Mark, *Newsletter Sourcebook.* Cincinnati, North Light Books, 1993. Uses a wide selection of newsletters to illustrate design issues, including type, graphics, color, and photos.
>
> Fanson, Barbara A., *Producing a First-Class Newsletter: A guide to planning, writing, editing, designing, photography, production, and printing.* North Vancouver, Self-Counsel Press, 1994. Content is summed up in the title; includes a number of useful worksheets.
>
> Floyd, Elaine, *Marketing with Newsletters: How to boost sales, add members & raise funds with a printed, faxed or Web-site newsletter,* Second edition. St Louis, Newsletter Resources, 1997. Focuses on editorial and graphic content in marketing newsletters.
>
> Floyd, Elaine, *Quick and easy newsletters: A step-by-step system using software you already have to create a newsletter in an afternoon.* St. Louis, Newsletter Resources, 1998.

Holden, Greg, *Official Online Marketing with Netscape Book: Build Your Business with the Power of Netscape.* Research Triangle Park, Netscape Press, 1996. How to create electronic marketing newsletters and distribute them on the Internet.

Hudson, Howard Penn, *Publishing Newsletters,* Revised Edition. New York, Charles Scribner's Sons, 1988. Includes editorial and design information, and deals extensively with subscription newsletters.

Kemper, Gary, W. "The Real Scoop: A study of employee publications finds a strong mismatch of CEO wants, employee interests, and actual content," *Industry Week.* (June 17, 1991): 67–69.

A number of other books about newsletters have been published – one recent online search generated more than two dozen of them. Some deal with specific topics, including church newsletters, desktop publishing, and design.

Online

Go to Wilson Internet Services at *http://www.wilsonweb.com* for an example of an effective online newsletter, *Web Marketing Today,* and a huge library of articles that addresses all aspects of Web marketing, including newsletters.

The about.com Guide to Newsletters at *http://publishing.about.com/arts/publishing/cs/newsletters/index.htm* covers both print and electronic publishing.

A Manager's Guide to Newsletters, the Web site, at *http://www.managersguide.com*

Communication, and persuasive communication

These resources deal with communication at an academic level, several of them as textbooks.

Hirsch, Eric Donald, *The Philosophy of Communication.* Chicago, The University of Chicago Press, 1977.

Katz, Elihu, Michael Gurevitch, and Hadassah Haas, "On the use of the mass media for important things," *American Sociological Review* 38 (April 1973):164–181.

Lewis, Phillip V., *Organizational Communication: The Essence of Effective Management,* Second Edition. Columbus, Grid Publishing Inc. 1980.

Littlejohn, Stephen W., *Theories of Human Communication,* Fourth Edition. Belmont, Wadsworth Publishing Company, 1992.

Reardon, Kathleen Kelley, *Persuasion in Practice.* Newbury Park, Sage Publications, 1991. Application of persuasion principles.

Smith, Mary John, *Persuasion and Human Action: A Review and Critique of Social Influence Theories.* Belmont, Wadsworth Publishing Company, 1982.

Tan, Alexis S., *Mass Communication Theories and Research*, Second Edition. New York, John Wiley & Sons, 1985.

Online

See the Web site of the International Association of Business Communicators, which publishes *IABC Communication World,* at *http://www.iabc.com*

Management

An enormous number of books about management – both academic and popular – are available. The following are a few that I have found particularly useful, both in writing this book and in managing businesses.

Drucker, Peter F., *Management: Tasks, Responsibilities, Practices.* New York, Harper & Row, Publishers, 1974. Still one of the best starting points for anyone who wants to understand modern management.

Peter, J. Paul and Jerry C. Olson, *Consumer Behavior: Marketing Strategy Perspectives.* Homewood, Irwin, 1987. A good textbook on the marketing sub-discipline of consumer behavior (sometimes also called consumer psychology).

Quinn, James Brian, Henry Mintzberg, and Robert M. James, *The Strategy Process: Concepts, Contexts, and Cases.* Englewood Cliffs, Prentice Hall, 1988. Surveys modern thinking about business strategy, and includes an extensive set of cases.

Ries, Al and Jack Trout, *Positioning: The Battle for Your Mind.* New York, Warner Books Edition, McGraw-Hill Inc., 1986. An influential and important book that deals with advertising and marketing from the viewpoint of consumer perceptions.

Wright, Peter, Mark J. Kroll, and John Parnell, *Strategic Management: Concepts and Cases.* Englewood Cliffs, Prentice Hall, 1996. Examination of strategy at the corporate, business, and functional levels.

Magazines

An extensive array of magazines covers just about every aspect of management. Important generalist publications include *Business Week, Fortune,* and *Industry Week.*

Online

Visit *http://www.asq.org* for the American Society for Quality, publisher of *Quality Progress* magazine. Its Web site is a good starting point for information and resources about Total Quality Management and Quality Assurance:

See *http://www.qca.org* for information about the Quality Council of Alberta, the successor organization to the Calgary Quality Council. The site also includes a good set of links to Quality-related resources.

Index

Ability
  customers 97
  employees 97
  members 97
  publishers 31, 55, 187, 192
  readers 64, 94, 97-98, 130, 191
    examples 67-69, 100
Actions 29, 39-40, 48, 51, 72, 75
Administration 2, 103-159, 178
Advertising 96, 187
Advise (voice)
  applications 86-88
  defined 84
  examples 88-91
  page count 98, 131
Allocation 99, 108, 112, 136
Amortization 135-136
Analyze (voice)
  applications 87-88
  defined 83
  evaluation 110
  page count 131
Annual
  budget 137
  plan 118-119
  planning 119
  reports 153
Annualize (budgeting) 136
Articles
  credibility of 62, 67
  ideas for 153-159
  media relations 141-142, 144
  relevant 61, 78
  sources 76, 150-151, 153
Assessment team 190
Assessments
  of newsletters 186-190
  of readers 85, 172-173, 186
  See also Evaluation
Assignments 108, 111, 113
Associations
  as content sources 154, 159
  costs and returns to 176, 182
  editorial boards for 114
  membership benefits 61, 75
  objectives of 1, 28, 44, 73, 184
Attitudes
  changing 82
  defined 40
  evaluation of 188
  examples 45-46, 90
  influencing 29, 39-40, 60, 63, 82
  page count and 131
  ranges of 43
  segmentation by 42, 164, 167
Backgrounding 142
Behaviors
  buyers' 75
  changing 29, 40, 82, 90
  co-workers' 75
  consistency of 63
  customers' 76
  defined 40
  evaluation of 188
  influencing 29, 60, 63, 76, 150
    examples 44, 46
  modelling 49
  ranges of 43
  reinforcing 40, 82
  segmentation by 164
Beliefs, *see* Attitudes
Benchmarks 186
Benefits
  employee 56, 77
  from newsletters 48, 50, 99, 192
  of editorial board service 114
  of media relations 140, 143
  vs. features 61-62
Book reviews 154
Boundaries, shared environment 74-75, 151
Break-even analysis 179
Break-even equation 179
Budget 135, 137
Budgets
  annual 137
  editorial board supervision 109
  evaluation of 192
  in annual planning 119
  in newsletter processes 118
  strategy for 130
  variances in 123
Calendar of events 154
Cartoons 154
Catalogs 154
Challenge (the voice)
  applications 86-88
  defined 83
Change (vs. reinforcement)
  and number of pages 98-99
  and shared environment 76
  examples 44, 46
  objectives 40

objectives for 40
Changes
    and demand for newsletters 29, 31
    and lower communication costs 31
    as a content source 154
    new objectives 188
    responsibility for 187
Characteristics, reader 82, 85, 164, 170
Checklist 119
Circulation 140
Commitment of publishers 55
Committees
    as content sources 151, 154
    editorial board 110, 113
    segmentation by 169
Communication
    control of 36
    for competitive advantage 35
    for internal development 32, 41
    frequency of 100
    in mass media 62
    motivation for 44
    objectives 135, 192
    of complex issues 41
    on editorial boards 106, 114
    strategy 108
    with stakeholders 1
Competitors
    and security of information 54
    as content sources 56, 153, 155
Compilations 155
Complex issues 32, 41, 74
Computers 31
    and newsletter feasibility 30
    budgeting for 134
Condensation of information
    as content 151-153
    defined 152
Consistency
    among members 95
    defined 63
    evaluation of 189-190
    examples 67-68, 89-91
    presentation tactics and 82
    ranges of 85
    voices for 87
Consult (voice)
    applications 86-88
    defined 83
    examples 88-91
Contact information 142
Content
    criteria for 72

evaluation 189
    examples 67, 69, 102
    macro approach 76, 78, 80
    micro approach 76, 78, 80, 152
    mass media 143
    planning for 118-119
    reader responses to 60, 85
    relevant 62, 75
    sources 153
    strategic 72
Contests 155
Context 33, 64-65, 142
Contributor guidelines 120
Control
    demand factors 33, 42
    mass media coverage 143
Cost per employee per issue 181
Cost per member per year 182
Costs
    and budgets 109, 133
    and newsletter popularity 29, 31
    and returns 176
    annual 183
    controlling 33
    frequency and 99
    mailing 178
    of communicating 31
    page count and 99
    per copy 178
    sources of 176
Credibility
    and shared environment 74
    evaluation of 189
    perceived 141
    relevance and 62, 74
Crossword puzzles 155
Customer newsletters
    see Marketing newsletters
Customers
    as content sources 151, 155
    complex issues and 32
    expectations of 32
    newsletter objectives for 38, 41
    on editorial boards 112-113
    segmentation of 168
Decision model 48, 50-51
Decision points 60, 64
Decision to publish 33
Delays in publishing 127
Demand factors
    decision to publish and 33
    defined 31
    evaluation of 187

examples 34
  in setting content boundaries 74
Demands on publishers 54
Demographics 42, 164-165, 169
Design 66, 135
Desktop publishing
  and newsletter popularity 30
  budgeting for 135
Direct costs per issue 136
Distribution 123
Economies of scale 178
Editorial
  concepts 135
  management 119
  policy 115
Editorial boards
  benefits of service on 114
  changing 115
  creating 112
  equity on 108
  evaluation of 191
  objectives of 112
  planning meetings 118
  policies governing 107
  profiling readers by 170
  recruiting for 114
  serving reader needs 53
  structure of 106
  supervising staff 109
  supporting staff 110
Editors
  and board policies 108
  and segmentation 167
  board membership 113
  budgeting for 135-136
  in evaluation process 191
  in mass media 140, 142-147
  independence of 115, 119
  knowing costs and returns 180
  mass media 148
  support for 106, 111-112
  using board policies 109
Elaboration and extension 155
Electronic newsletters, see Internet
Emotion
  affecting willingness 63
  evaluation of 189-190
  examples 67-68, 89, 91
  for persuasion 29
  presentation tactics and 82
  ranges of 85
  voices for 86
Empathize (voice)

  applications 87
  defined 83
Employee newsletters
  content 77
  cost per employee per issue 181
  costs and returns measures 177
  editorial board representation 113-114
  evaluation of 186, 189
  examples
    ability 67
    decision factors 34
    frequency 99
    Inside News 6
    objectives 46
    page count 100
    presentation 89
    reader needs 56
    shared environment 79
    willingness 67
  frequency 132
  hours per employee per issue 181
  measuring costs and returns 176
  micro/macro content 76
  multiple purposes 184
  need for 32
  objectives of 76
  reader ability 97
  reader profiles 164
  reader willingness 64, 95
  segmentation for 165, 168
  shared environment 73-74
  size of print run 132
  target audiences 164
  wrong subjects for 75
Employees
  as content sources 151, 155
  cost per employee per issue 181
  development of 32, 41
  editorial board representation 106
  hours per employee per issue 181
  needs 53
  new expectations of 32
  newsletter priorities 77
  objectives of 53
  productivity 182
  representation on editorial boards 112
Entertain (voice)
  applications 86-87
  defined 83
Envision (voice)
  applications 86-88
  defined 83
  examples 90

Evaluation 161-192
  by editorial boards 109-110
  criteria for 187
  defined 2
  in annual planning 119
  measures 186
  of consumption experiences 50
  of development costs 135
  of mass media priorities 145
  periodic 186
  process 118, 123
  reader's consumption experience 52
  responsibility for changes 187
  setting new objectives 192
Excerpts 156
Expansion of information
  as content 152-153
  defined 152
Expectations 32, 34, 41, 74
Explicit, vs. implicit messages 66
Exposures 96, 190
Fact checking 109, 112
Faxletter, Calgary Quality Council 23
  decision factors 35
  frequency 100
  introduction to 7
  objectives 44
  page count 101
  presentation tactics 90
  reader needs 56
  reader willingness and ability 67
  shared environment 77
Fixed costs 177, 179, 183-184
Frequency
  and cost calculations 99
  based on willingness 94
  evaluation of 190
  examples 99-101
  in budgeting 133
  most common schedules 95
  of electronic newsletters 96
  of printed newsletters 95
  segmentation by 168
  strategy for 99
Full cost-per-issue budget 138
Goals 189
  editorial board 115
  employee and employer 95
  for newsletter distribution 133
  in newsletter planning 119
  newsletter usage and 48
  organizational 1, 39, 43, 77, 106
  personal

  defined 48
  envisioning 83
  evaluation of 188
  knowledge of 53
  relevance to 61
  shared environment 73
  use of mass media and 28
  wrong subjects to achieve 75
Governance 110
Government reports 156
Grammar-checking 65, 119-120, 125
Hours per employee per issue 181
How many copies? 132
How many pages? 130
How much will it cost? 133
How often? 132
Implicit, vs. explicit messages 66
Industry Week 77, 198
Influence
  as persuasion 29
  attitudes and behaviors 40
  frequency and 95-96
  in newsletter definition 54
  involvement factor 62
  media relations and 140-141, 145
  of member newsletters 132
  readers 53
  shared environment and 72, 74, 76, 150
  stakeholders 28
  through design 88
  through rhetoric 66
  two-step strategy and 45
  voices for 82
Inform, *see* Advise
Inside News 15
  decision factors 34
  frequency 99
  introduction to 6
  objectives 46
  page count 100
  presentation 89
  reader needs 56
  shared environment 79
  willingness and ability 66
Interactivity 67
  See also Involvement
Internal development 32, 41
Internet
  as content source 156
  electronic newsletters 31, 96, 132, 177
  persuasion model 54
Interpret (voice)
  applications 86-88

defined 84
examples 88-90
Interpreting (media relations) 142
Involvement
　as a reader characteristic 85
　defined 62
　evaluation of 189-190
　examples 68, 88-90
　presentation tactics for 82
　ranges of 85
　voices for 85
Layout Activities 121
Level of abstraction 64-65, 68
Line art 156
Lists 156
Macro approach to content 76, 78, 80
Magazines 140, 156
Mailing costs 178
Mailing list management 148
Management
　accounting 176
　and editorial boards
　　benefits 114
　　changes 115
　　evaluation 191
　　evaluation of operations 110
　　policies 109
　　representation on 113
　　style 107
　approvals 108-109
　as a development cost 135-136
　as content source 153
　publisher as 73
　responsibility for changes 187
　segmentation by 168
　shared environment and 73, 75, 150
Managerial questions 1
Managers
　as content sources 151, 157
　as media contacts 142
　as media sources 143
　credibility of 67, 69
　evaluation responsibilities 192
　internal development of 32
　on editorial boards 106, 109, 114-115
　profiling by 170
　setting objectives 41, 99
　shared environment and 73
　understanding costs and returns 180
Margin contribution, segmentation by 168
Market research 164
Marketing newsletters
　break-even analysis 179

　budgeting for 132
　buyer willingness and 94
　complex issues in 32
　content sources for 159
　costs and returns 176, 180
　delays 127
　editorial board representation 113
　examples
　　decision factors 36
　　frequency 101
　　objectives 45
　　page count 101
　　presentation 88
　　reader needs 55
　　shared environment 78
　　The Sovereign Report 5
　　willingness and ability 68
　fixed and variable costs 177
　frequency 96, 132
　micro/macro content 76
　objectives 41, 191
　profiling readers 164
　reader ability 97
　reader willingness 64
　return on investment 176
　segmentation for 42, 168
　shared environment of 73-75
　targeting readers 42, 164
Measures, for evaluation 186
Media
　attention 143
　choices 28, 41, 187
　electronic newsletters 96
　monitoring mass media 146
　niches 143
Media relations
　execution 146
　getting attention 143
　priorities 145
　specialty media 147
Medium/media/mass media 193
Members
　and newsletter strategies 183-184
　as content sources 151
　demands on publishers 54
　evaluating participation of 186
　motivating 44
　new expectations of 32
　prospective 183
　segmentation of 169
　shared environment and 73-74, 150
　willingness of 64
Membership newsletters

ability of readers 97
budgeting for 132
content sources for 151
cost per member per year 183
costs and returns measures 176, 183, 186
editorial board representation 113
evaluation of 189
examples
   Calgary Quality Council Faxletter 7
   decision factors 35
   frequency 100-101
   objectives 44
   presentation 90
   reader needs 56
   shared environment 77
   willingness and ability 67
frequency 132
micro/macro content 76
segmentation for 168
shared environment of 73-74
target audiences 164
willingness of readers 64, 95
Micro approach to content 76, 78, 80, 152
Mission 2, 38-39
Multi-purpose newsletter 184
Multiple objectives 43
Multiple segmentation 169
New products 157
Newsletter loop 51, 60, 64
Newsletters
   benefits of publishing 51
   current popularity of 29-31, 33
   decision factors for 33-34
   defined 54
   demands on publishers 54
   electronic 96, 130, 132-133, 159
   examples 4
   function of 1-2, 28-29
   scheduling 125
   strategic 29, 38, 72
   See also Employee newsletters, Marketing newsletters, and Membership newsletters
Newspapers 28, 140
Niche audiences
   and demand for newsletters 32
   defined 164
   examples 34
   publishing decision and 41
   shared environment and 74
Number of copies (budgeting) 133
Number of pages, *see* Page count
Objectives
   and evaluation 188, 192

editorial board 112
evaluation criteria for 186
examples 44
for media relations 140
organizational 1-3
personal 85
publisher 52, 72, 96, 99, 119
reader 48-50, 94, 188
setting 43
Office space (budgeting) 134
Operations 107, 110
Owners 158
Page count
   ability and 94, 98
   examples 100-101
   in budgeting 133
   reinforce vs. change 98
Peripherals, computer 30-31
Persuasion
   as a mass media function 28
   defined 29
   need for 28
   newsletters for 38-39, 54
   objectives for 40
   reader response to 54
   right content for 189
   shared environment and 75
Persuasion in Practice 29, 199
Photos 157
Planning 118-119
Policies
   editorial board 106-107, 110, 191
   planning 118
Popularity of newsletters 29
Positioning 33, 38
Presentation
   evaluation of 189
   examples 88
   page count and 98
   planning for 118
Previous articles 158
Print run, size of 132
Printed newsletters 98, 130, 132, 177, 184
Printing costs 178
Printing, preparation for 122
Problem solving, *see* Solve
Procedures, editorial board 107
Processes
   budgeting 109, 130
   content development 151
   decision making 50
   defined 194
   evaluation of 186-187

measuring costs and returns 176
profiling 164
proofreading 121
publishing 118
scheduling 125
segmentation 169
setting objectives 43
thought 40
Productivity 97, 181-182, 186
Profiling readers 85
Profit 179
Promotion 39, 140
Proofread 119-120, 124
Proofreaders 121
Proofreading process 121
Proximity 33
Psychographics 42, 164-165, 167, 173
Publicity 140
Publishers
  as persuaders 29
  belief consistency with readers 87
  benefits to 48, 50
  budgeting by 130
  building positive emotions 86
  consistency of belief with readers 85
  credibility of 62
  demands on 54
  in newsletter definition 54
  objectives 44, 72
  segmentation strategies of 168, 173
  shared environment and 72-73, 150, 189
  voices used by 85
Publishing (newsletters)
  control 33, 143
  decision factors 33, 41
  delays 127
  feasibility 29, 31
  fixed and variable costs 177
  for internal development 32
  for niche audiences 164
  newsletter loop 39
  objectives 43
  process 118
  supply and demand factors 30
Purposes
  of voices 82
  strategic newsletters 38
Puzzle books 157
Radio 28, 54, 140, 147
Readability 64-66, 120, 125
Reader profiling
  process 169
  segmentation and 165

Readers
  characteristics of 164
  cost of reaching 31
  diversity of 46
  in the newsletter loop 39
  influencing 1, 28-29
  needs of 48, 53-54, 62, 188
  responses 38-40, 44, 188
  targeted 42
    and objectives 43
    evaluation of responses 186
    receiving vs. reading 60
    segmentation process 170
    selecting 164
Reading competence 64-65, 68
Reardon, Kathleen Kelley 29, 199
Reason 29
Recruiting
  budgeting for 134
  editorial boards 114
  members 184
Reinforce (vs. change)
  as an objective 40, 76
  attitudes 40
  behaviors 40
  defined 40
  evaluation 188
  examples 44
  page count and 98
Relationships
  board and readers 107
  board and staff 110
  costs and returns 176
  demographics and responses 42
  newsletter and organization 2
  objectives and resources 188
  publisher and reader 48, 51
  with mass media 140
Relevance
  defined 61-62
  evaluation of 189
  examples 67, 69
  in media relations 143, 145
  required for teaching 84
  shared environment and 74-75
Repetition 141
Reporters 140, 142-145
Reports 152-153, 156, 158, 166
Reprints 156
Research reports 158
Resources 153
Responses
  ability of readers and 97

advertising theory of 96
categorizing 40
evaluation of 190
reader 38-39, 41, 74, 179
role of relevance in 61
segmenting for 42
to persuasion 29
voices for 82
willingness factor and 82
Responsibilities
editorial board 106, 111, 114
for evaluation 186-187
in annual planning 119
Retrospectives 158
Return on newsletter investment 176, 186
Revenue 176, 179-180
Rewrites 158
Rhetoric 66
Schedules
annual plan 119
each issue 119
editorial board contributions 111
in budgeting 135
Segmentation
applied 169
by objectives 42
by reader needs 53
defined 32, 164
demographics 165
evaluation of 188
multiple 169
of fixed and variable costs 183
other approaches 168
psychographics 167
strategies 165
Selecting an audience 42
Service requirements, segmentation by 168
Sets of characteristics 85
Setup charges 178
Shared environment 79
boundaries of 74, 76
defined 72-73
evaluation of 189
examples 77-79
link to relevance and credibility 74
reviewed 150
Shareholders 158
Software 30-31
Solve (voice)
applications 86-88
defined 84
examples 88-91
page count 131

Sources of article ideas 153
Sovereign Report, see *The Sovereign Report*
Specialty media 147
Spelling worksheet 119, 124
Spending
budgeting tactics 130
editorial board supervision of 111
Spin-off articles 158
Staff 110, 115, 191
Stakeholders
as content sources 151
cost of communicating with 31
defined 1, 195
new expectations of 32, 41, 74
on editorial boards 110, 112
persuading 38
Startup plan 118
Stories, sources 153
Strategic
alliances 67
approach to content 72
clarity 127
communication 192
issues and budgeting 130
newsletters 29, 38, 54
Strategy 26-56
defined 2
evaluation of 187-188
implementation of 107
marketing 42
newsletter planning 118
two-step 45
Structure 64
Style sheets 119
Subscription newsletters 32
Success and failure criteria 109
Supervision 109, 118, 191
Suppliers 159
Supply and demand factors 30, 33
Support of editorial staff 106, 119, 191
Syndication services 159
Tactical clarity 127
Tactical issues and budgeting 130
Tactics 57-102
defined 2
editorial board 107, 110
planning 118
presentation 82
Tasks
of editorial boards 106, 115, 191
of editorial staff 108
scheduling 125
Teach (voice)

applications 86, 88
defined 84
examples 89-91
Technology 29-32
Television 28, 140
Terms of reference (editorial board) 107
Text structure 66
The Sovereign Report 9
  decision factors 36
  frequency 101
  introduced 5
  objectives 45
  page count 101
  presentation styles 88
  reader needs 55
  scheduling 128
  shared environment 78
  willingness and ability 68
Thoughts, *see* Attitudes
Timelines for objectives 39
Trade associations 159
Trade periodicals 159
Training, budgeting for 134
Trends 29
Two-step communication strategy 44
Uncertainty, and willingness to respond 94
Unions 159
Unique source 151
Variable costs 177, 179, 183-184
Voices 82-88, 98, 130, 189
Volume, segmentation by 168
Willingness
  examples 67-68
  of employees 95
  of publishers 54
  of readers 63, 82, 94-96, 132, 189-190
Word processors 30
World Wide Web 156
  See also Internet
Writers 41, 66, 111
Year end 159

About the author

Robert F. Abbott, M.B.A., founded and owns The Newsletter Company, which has served a select group of clients in Calgary, Canada since 1991. He has had wide-ranging work and managerial experience, including 10 years as a radio news writer and announcer. In addition, he participates in many public service activities.

Mr. Abbott also publishes his own newsletter, one that helps managers, professionals, and others use communication to achieve or advance toward their objectives. *Abbott's Communication Letter,* a free publication, is distributed by email. Read about it, see sample issues, and subscribe at *http://www.abbottletter.com* .

Your questions and comments about *A Manager's Guide to Newsletters: Communicating for Results,* newsletters, or communication are always welcomed. Send an email message to *abbottr@managersguide.com* .

Manager's Guide site on the Internet

http://www.managersguide.com

You can visit the Manager's Guide site online by going to the following World Wide Web address: *http://www.managersguide.com/*

www.ingramcontent.com/pod-product-compliance
Lightning Source LLC
Chambersburg PA
CBHW081215230426
43666CB00015B/2737